Ernst Pauer

Musical Forms

Vocal and Instrumental, Sacred and Secular

Ernst Pauer

Musical Forms
Vocal and Instrumental, Sacred and Secular

ISBN/EAN: 9783337084677

Printed in Europe, USA, Canada, Australia, Japan

Cover: Foto ©Thomas Meinert / pixelio.de

More available books at **www.hansebooks.com**

Musical Forms..

Vocal and Instrumental
Sacred and Secular

By ...
ERNEST PAUER

INTRODUCTORY REMARKS.

It is a common remark that musical amateurs talk of different musical forms with a very vague and uncertain notion of their meaning. It cannot be denied that in this respect musical instruction is deficient, when compared, for instance, with the study of the different forms of poetry, respecting which, in general, our knowledge is more precise and accurate. And yet our delightful musical art by no means owes its existence to mere accident and chance; many illustrious men have devoted their best energy and closest attention to the consolidation of that wonderfully organized structure which we may well be proud to recognize in musical writing. Neither can it be denied that the taste for music is innate in a greater number of people than that for painting, sculpture, and poetry; and it might almost be assumed that people sang before they spoke, and that for this reason Music may justly be called the oldest art, although in regard to development and perfection it is the most modern. The very general distribution of musical talent by bountiful nature amongst all classes of human society may in some measure account for the absence of technical knowledge of the different musical forms. An accurate acquaintance, however, with the essential conditions and the necessary structure of a certain piece, will undoubtedly tend to a just appreciation of the degree of merit it contains; and consequently will help to form a just estimate of its composer. My purpose is to explain, in this little book, the respective forms of Vocal and Instrumental Music, and at the same time to point out what composers have excelled in each of these forms.

I beg to thank the Rev. T. Helmore, M.A., Chaplain-in-Ordinary to the Queen, for kindly revising and supplementing the Sacred Forms of Vocal Music.

E. PAUER.

3, Onslow Houses, London, S.W., 1878.

TABLE OF CONTENTS.

INTRODUCTORY REMARKS.

FORM IN MUSIC.

Form—Accent—Metre—Rhythm—Style—Figure—Melody—The Period and its construction—Thematic work.

FORM WITH REGARD TO THE RELATION OF SEPARATE PARTS OF POLYPHONIC MUSIC.

Counterpoint—Double Counterpoint—Fugue—Canon.

MUSICAL FORMS.

(Forms of Movements, etc., of Musical Works.)

VOCAL MUSIC.

I.—SACRED FORMS.

Antiphony—Hymn—Ambrosian Hymn—Anthem—Motet—Mass or Requiem—Introit—Gradual—Offertory—Stabat Mater—Miserere—Lamentations—Canticum (Magnificat)—Lauda Sion Salvatorem—Laudes—Laudes Episcopi—Laudi spirituali—Oratorio—Passion-Music—Choral—The Figured Choral—Psalms—Psalmody—Concerto da chiesa.

FORMS BELONGING TO SACRED AND SECULAR VOCAL MUSIC.

Recitative—Aria—Arietta—Arioso—Cavata—Cavatina—Coloratura—Duet—Dialogue—Chorus—Cantata—Cantatina—Quodlibet.

II.—SECULAR FORMS.

Song—Chanson—Maggiolata—Ballad—National Songs—Couplet—Madrigal—Glee—Rounds and Catches—Obsolete Forms of Songs—Pastoral—Liederspiel—Masque—Burletta—Opera—Intermedium—Intermezzo.

TABLE OF CONTENTS.

INSTRUMENTAL MUSIC.

Introductory remarks—*Older forms of instrumental music:*—Prelude (Voluntary)—Toccata—Invention—Ricercata—Fugue—Symphony—Intrade—Concerto grosso—Aria with or without doubles—Ground—Suite—Partita.

I.—CYCLICAL FORMS.

Sonata—String quartet—Cassazione—Serenade—Divertimento—Notturno—Symphony—Concerto—Concertino—Concertstück—Overture.

II.—SINGLE FORMS.

Fantasia—Caprice—Capriccio—Scherzo—The Variation—March—Songs without words—Etude (Study)—Idyll—Eclogue—Villanella—Rhapsody—Impromptu—Intermezzo—Sketch (Esquisse, Skizze), Potpourri, Quodlibet, Mélange, Pasticcio.

DANCE MUSIC.

I.—OLD DANCES.

Allemande—Courante (Corrente)—Bourrée—Gavotte—Cebell—Sarabande—Gigue—Angloise—Brawl—Chaconne—Minuet—Passacaglio—Passamezzo—Passepied—Pavan—Galliard—Rigaudon—Siciliano—The old dance movements classified with respect to their time and rhythmical expression.

II.—MODERN AND NATIONAL DANCES.

German dances—English dances—Norwegian and Swedish dances—Wallachian, Moldavian and Roumanian dances—Italian dances—Spanish dances—French dances—Bohemian dances—Russian dances—Polish dances—Hungarian dances—Concluding remarks.

APPENDIX.

Melodrama—Monodrama—Duodrama—Chamber-Music—Drawing-room Music—Descriptive Music: I. Tone-painting; II. Programme-Music—Robert Schumann's Fancy-Pieces—Obsolete forms.

MUSICAL FORMS.

FORM IN MUSIC.

FORM.

Music, when portraying feelings or emotions, assumes various forms and undergoes various modifications; and, being the representation of a *passing* feeling or emotion, has a definite outline, a commencement, development, and ending.

As feelings of a very different nature are sometimes developed in a very uniform way, one and the same musical form—for instance, aria or sonata—may have the same general outlines, and yet express very various feelings, because the style of the movement may present great varieties within the same boundaries. But all feeling must associate itself with certain mental ideas to obtain a concrete existence, for without relation to an object it would not even realize its general intention as pleasure or pain; neither love nor hatred is felt, unless it is excited by some object; but the feelings are modified in the most various ways by the nature and construction of the object or impulse, and by the co-operation of various circumstances. But with all the freedom that is thus allowed, the form into which musical sounds are moulded must be sufficiently precise to direct the attention of the hearer and awaken in him the impression of a definite and distinct idea. Such ideas cannot, however, be entirely individual and special: in their nature they must be general—a kind of reflex of what we imagine to have been the intention of the composer, except where the music is associated with the text, which gives a more accurate definition to our conceptions. For instance, a musical composition can very well awaken in us the idea of a hero, but hardly of an individual hero, unless other circumstances assist our general feeling. For musical form, after all, must be based upon natural laws, and in the end is but the reproduction in tone-language of the feeling in the mind of the composer, who (sometimes philosophically, as with Beethoven; sometimes instinctively, as with Haydn) expresses that feeling according to a rule based upon nature and reason.

ACCENT.

Accent is a stress laid upon certain notes in a series with two separate effects. In the first instance the accented notes merely bind the others into definite groups; in the second instance they produce a particular and strengthened expression. The former of these constitutes the *grammatical* or *metrical*, the latter the *oratorical* accent.

Grammatical accentuation is the fundamental and natural one, which no ordered sequence of tone can dispense with, for without it the sequence would lack organic cohesion in reference to measure of time, and would, accordingly, be unintelligible.

Oratorical accentuation is not an artificial one in contrast to the former, the natural one, for both must agree in their essence and may not stand in contradiction to each other; and its main features, a correct oratorical accentuation, must at all times likewise be a correct grammatical one, in spite of certain freedoms allowed for the sake of particular expression. Yet it extends beyond the simple regularity of the grammatical order of accent, and appears as a higher and artistically free development, forming an essential element of expressive performance. A passage may be played with perfectly correct grammatical accentuation, and yet in a very stiff and expressionless manner, where the vivifying power of the oratorical accentuation is wanting. With the latter, however, we have less to do here than with the grammatical system of accents, of time and its components.

1. *The Grammatical Accent.*—This may be most practically illustrated in the following manner. Let the reader imagine to himself a series of pulsations or beats without any order or regulated sequence, following each other quite monotonously, and, whether they unite together into a confused noise or are separately audible, exhibiting nothing that could represent a division or a grouping that would result from certain resemblances recurring at stated intervals; such a sequence of pulsations would be inorganic and unintelligible. But slightly removed above this would be a series of entirely regular pulsations, following each other without any kind of change; such a sequence would show only a mechanical order without any inner life, and is just as uninteresting and unattractive as if we were to place instead of it merely the *time-signature*. By a natural impulse, however, we could hardly imagine or bear such a sequence of pulsations without dividing it into certain definite groups, to give life and attraction to it, and this would be done according to a higher rule of order, involving the resemblance of each of these groups to the rest with regard to the regularity of their sequence. Our natural feeling for recurrence or periodicity would form these groups by giving prominence to the first beat or pulsation of each group of a certain number of beats by a greater stress. This stress is the accent, and the group of pulsations over which it dominates constitutes the musical *metre*, the time. The accent gives connection to the whole series of beats by bringing the separate members of the series into definite relation with each other, for without it, they have no connection with or reference to each other; each one is isolated and has no relation to its predecessors or successors; each is a beginning without a continuation. But the accentuated beat involves the expectation that it will be succeeded by an unaccented one, as the unaccented beat, on the other hand, prepares us to expect an accented one to follow. The duration of the unaccented beat is fixed according to the preceding accentuated one.

Such a group of several notes, consisting of alternate accented and unaccented members, is really only the order to which the higher rhythmical life of the melody must be subject, so that its various parts may be recognizable, and, through the alternation of rise and fall, may become manifold and animated; this is no longer an outward mechanical division, but real development; the beats are evolved from one another; each is the consequence of its predecessor and, again, the cause of its immediate successor. Such an intimate connection, however, is only possible in a series of beats, arranged in the simplest manner, in which a single rise follows a separate fall, as in the following example—

but this simple sequence of an alternate rise and fall is sufficient for the formation of the different metres, even for the triple time, as we shall see; it must also be remembered at the outset that our musical accent is not bound to any specific duration of the sound, and exerts the same influence whether it falls on a long note or on quite a short one.

The Bar and its Accentuation.—The bar may be considered as a recurrence of a certain number of beats, identical in duration, the first of these beats in each group having always the principal accent, while the others are accented less strongly or not at all. In notation these equal groups are separated by perpendicular lines, called bar lines—

but it is not the bar-line that defines the bar, but the accent: the bar-line is only an arrangement for the easier comprehension of the whole rhythmical and metrical division of the melody. The first beat of the bar, which has the chief accent, is called *thesis*, or the downward beat, or the strong and heavy position; the unaccented is called *arsis*, the raising, the upward beat, or the weak, light position. In the Latin and Greek metrical science, however, we find the meaning of arsis and thesis reversed; arsis, the raising of the voice or of the foot in marking, being considered as the strong—thesis, the falling of the voice or foot, the weak position. In this acceptation the words are also used by some musical authors; therefore, setting aside the words arsis and thesis, it is better to keep close to the idea of the strong position as associated with the downward, and the weak position with the upward beat.*

In the division of the beats of a bar there occur, besides the chief accent that marks the whole bar, other accents of a subordinate kind. It is well known that in music every length can be divided into any number of shorter lengths, equivalent to it in their sum. The kind of note according to which the time is named, for instance, the crotchets in 2-4 time, the quavers in 6-8, must be called divisions (members) of time; the smaller notes of different kinds into which these members can be broken up form the subdivision. When the members of the bar are resolved into a number of subdivisions, the

---

* This point is critically explained in detail in Stainer and Barrett's "Dictionary of Musical Terms," pp. 37-38, Article "Arsis."

same condition of falling and rising which combines the divisions is repeated on a smaller scale in the subdivisions. If we divide the members of the following bars, which are marked as a duple time—

into a number of subdivisions corresponding to it in value, for instance, into quavers—

or into semiquavers—

the claim of periodicity is felt in these smaller subdivisions, and divides the subordinate parts by means of secondary accents of a lower grade into similar groups, with an alternate rise and fall, like the whole series of crotchet beats in the larger form through the chief accent:—

In the foregoing accentuation the grouping of the subordinate parts has been accomplished, but the fundamental series of crotchet beats is still unrecognizable, because not defined by an especial accent. To make this series of beats intelligible an accent of the next higher grade is necessary, through which every two pairs of subordinate members are united into a division of the next higher order:—

So far as the two divisions of the bar are concerned, the crotchets should have the divisional accent in addition to their own accent as members of a subdivision, and are distinguished by a double weight from the simply accented subdivisions. The crotchet beats are now recognizable, but are not yet united, that is to say, they are not yet distinguished as thesis and arsis of the bar, for they have both only the same subordinate accent. The beat in the larger measure still appears monotonous, without connection, and not yet recognizable as the two-four time. Accordingly a further grouping is necessary, which is effected by the *chief* or *time*-accent of the first class, given to the first division of every complete bar:—

The time-accent, therefore, marks the time and divides the whole series into a number of groups, each containing an equal number of beats. The divisional accent of the second class marks the divisions of time, in contradistinction to their subordinate division, and the accent of the subordinate divisions unites these latter into groups of alternate falling and rising, as the second accent unites the subordinate pairs and the time-accent the chief divisions. If we draw together the semiquavers of the foregoing example, the order of accent is contracted in the following manner:—

The first crotchet of every bar has the principal or time-accent, the second crotchet has the secondary accent, in reference to its subordinate part; the third accent (that of the subordinate division) has vanished in the absence of a division into semiquavers. The same thing happens with the secondary accent, when the quavers are drawn together into crotchets:—

Thus this order of accent, originating with the separation of beats into bars, extends over all the greater and smaller divisions. It need hardly be observed, however, that these accents, and very frequently the time-accent also, are not always marked in the performance; on the other hand, in many cases the expressive declamatory execution of the melody requires an audible emphasizing of the second and tertiary divisions. Invariable rules cannot be given in this matter, but an educated artistic taste will recognize what should be done in each separate case.

We have now to turn to common time. This consists of four distinct divisions, and not of two contracted bars of two divisions each, changed into one of four divisions by the omission of the bar-line that parted them. Its system of accent can be easily recognized on the principle explained in reference to the two-four time. If we imagine the crotchets of a bar in common time (C), divided into semiquavers, the first semiquaver of each couple of semiquavers would have the accent of the third class—

the first semiquaver of each crotchet would have the accent of the second class:—

as only a *single* rise can follow each separate fall, the third crotchet as well as the first has a distinctive accent of the higher order, whereby the second and fourth crotchet become a rising inflection in contradistinction to these other two accents; thus they are *weak* parts of the time as opposed to the others, which are *strong*:—

Beyond this the first member of the bar has the bar accent which marks the rise or fall of the whole series in general:—

If this division is contracted—

there remains for the first note of the bar the chief accent, but for the third also a *weaker* accent, which the bar requires on account of its breadth, as three unaccented notes cannot be attached to a single accented one; but the fact that the secondary accent is weaker than the chief accent distinguishes the real common-time bar (C $\frac{4}{4}$) from two contracted two-four bars:—

The double fall and rise gives it weight and breadth, the diminished strength of the second, in comparison with the first, gives variety with regularity.

A bar of three members ($\frac{3}{2}$, $\frac{3}{4}$, $\frac{3}{8}$, triple time) has a chief accent; but as only one unaccented member is regulated by an accent, it has also a weaker secondary accent in the second member. If we represent a three-four bar in quavers, each first member of the three pairs of quavers has the secondary accent, and the first quaver of the bar has the principal accent in addition:—

If these quavers are contracted into crotchets the third crotchet transfers its accent to the second; which, however, as it already has a secondary accent of its own, would appear too weighty with a double one, and, therefore, throws back one accent upon the first crotchet, keeping the other for itself, as follows:—

The last crotchet of the bar is thus entirely without an accent, completely weak, but the second cannot be altogether unaccented, as it is the first number of a pair (the second and third crotchets), and has the secondary accent in reference to the third crotchet. But this accent of the second crotchet can only be weak because it is attached as arsis to the thesis of the bar. An entirely similar order of accents is seen where the members are divided into groups of three:—

Of these groups each concluding note is entirely without accent, the middle one has the tertiary accent, in relation to the third as the first member of a pair; every member of the bar as it consists of several parts has the secondary accent with reference to its parts, but that of the second group has a stronger accent than that of the third, as the first member of the second group comprising the bar. The first member of the bar has the bar accent in addition.

Thus the plain sequence of a rise after a fall is the foundation of all arrangement of accent. In the same way all descriptions of time are only derivations from the two-four, three-four, and common time; thus the six-four or six-eight in its fundamental form is a two-fold or a three-fold time, according to the accent given—

and the nine-four, nine-eight, is a three-fold; the twelve-four, twelve-eight, twelve-sixteen, twenty-four-sixteen, a four-fold one.

Transposition of the Accent.—For the sake of special effect a deviation often takes place from the established order of the accent by transposing it. The accent is transferred from the thesis to the nearest arsis: there are various kinds of transpositions of accent, but all are based on the same principle—namely, that the accent is moved from the thesis to the arsis, the latter obtaining the stress, while the former loses its weight. (Ex. I.) Very frequently this accentuation occurs when the note that has the arsis is longer than the thesis note. (Ex. II.)

But this transition of the accent must not continue too long, for if so, the accented arsis would usurp the place of the thesis and would no longer be intelligible merely as a transposition. For if the following line—

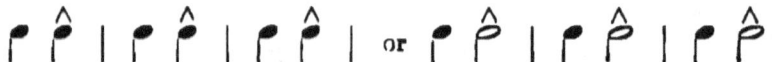

were long continued, our rhythmical instinct would very soon reduce this transposition of the accent to a natural simple order of accent by receiving the accentuated arsis as the thesis, because the natural and universal always asserts itself over the artificial and the special:—

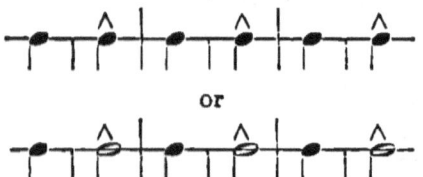

Two orders of accents, of which the one is natural and the other the transposition, may encounter at the same time:—

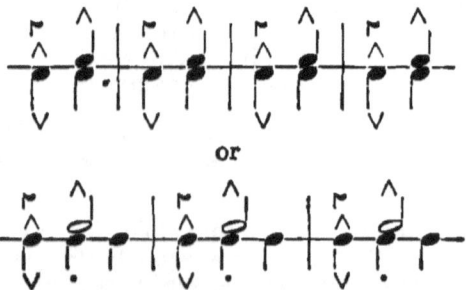

In the former of these last two examples each of the two members of the bar has a heavy accent, and such *marcato* figures may be very

effective in places where a very weighty emphasis is required. Still they cannot be used for any length of time together, as they would become heavy and cumbersome. The accentuation on the second example, with the accent on the first and second crotchets of the three-four bar, is sufficiently general; but then the accent on the first member is generally taken somewhat lighter as a secondary accent—

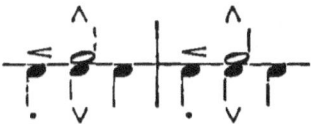

and the figure is in fact only an inversion of chief accent and secondary accent in the three-four bar—

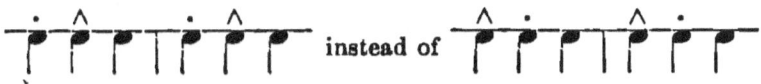

The secondary accent of the three-four bar is transposed from the second member to the third; thus instead of—

the third member thus appears as a stronger up-beat in preparation for the next bar.

The bar of two members is mingled with that of three members, the so-called *tempo rubato* (stolen time):—

The two-four (2/4) time mingles with the three-four (3/4), but in another manner. Three two-four (2/4) bars occupy the place of two three-four (3/4) bars:—

In reality these three two-four bars, which may also appear divided into members of bars, are nothing more than a three-four bar, the value of whose notes has been doubled, to give them weight and emphasis. Such passages are firmly accented and somewhat broadly enunciated, and occur in phrases of three-four time, and lively movements, generally towards the conclusion of a piece. Especially with the older composers, we find this kind of transposition frequently enough, generally in the form of three imperfect breves (◻) in the *tempus perfectum* instead of two perfect ones. In Handel's works (as "Susannah," St. John's Passion, etc.) it is found frequently enough, and also in six-eight time. From our present music, this very effective declamatory and rhythmical turn has almost entirely vanished.

Syncopè is the union of a thesis and arsis into a member of a bar wherein the accent is pushed forward from the thesis to the arsis, which was originally unaccented:—

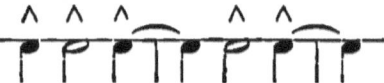

In this syncopation the second and fourth members are accented instead of the first and third. But as a separate rhythmical sequence syncopè soon ceases to be intelligible as a transposition, because, as in the former case, the accented arsis is soon understood by feeling as a thesis. If a syncopè is to maintain itself for any time as a pure unison, it must be interrupted in bars or in longer intervals by an accented thesis, which always recalls the natural accent to the memory:—

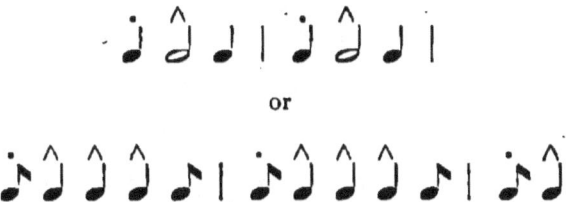

or

But where the syncopè occurs, as it usually does in a passage where there are various voices, it can be continued at pleasure without becoming unintelligible, because the other voices always meet it with the counterpoise of the natural order of accent:—

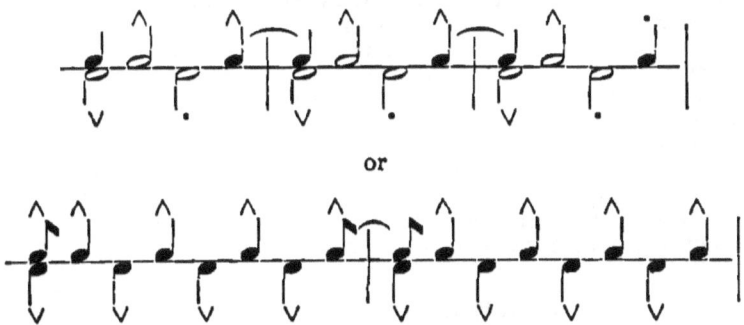

Usually all the members of the syncopè, as well as the more weakly accented or entirely unaccented members of the natural run of accents are strongly marked in order to make the opposition of the two orders of accents more strongly felt. It depends, however, upon the expression the passage is to have, for a soft or flowing character may be indicated by such an intermingling of the two systems of accents, in which case the decided marking, but not the accentuation, is omitted. Moreover, the term "syncopè" is also employed to designate every kind of attachment of a strong (or heavy) member of a bar to a weak (or light) one, even if the accent is not removed; thus in suspensions the thesis is attached to the arsis without any alteration of the order of accent.

The bound or *legato* suspension, even when it is not marked and more strongly expressed, always exhibits itself as a thesis, and is resolved as an arsis:—

The discord is always accentuated; its preparation and solution are unaccented. The conclusions always fall on an accented member of the bar, which need not, however, always be the first in the bar, but in common time may be the third, and through the deferred accent (in the three-four time only) may be the second. But in any case it must be a member of the bar, bearing an accent in reference to the other members.

In vocal compositions the accented syllables of the text or the emphasized words must always fall on the accented notes of the music, and it will be understood that in syncopation the spoken accent moves with the musical note. To put unaccented syllables to accented notes, or the reverse, is a twisting of language, and may be reckoned among the greatest errors of taste that a vocal composer can commit.

2. *Oratorical Accent.*—By oratorical accent we understand a certain declamatory character imparted to a performance by the emphasizing of certain parts, the procedure being founded on the natural system of accentuation. As in reciting a piece of poetry the effect would be lame and flat if the speaker were to rigidly adhere to the metre, so in a vocal or instrumental performance a pedantic maintenance of rhythm and accent would result in sameness and monotony. A certain license is therefore allowed to the performer, whose taste should indicate what parts of the composition may be emphasized to give a greater meaning to the whole; but great care must be taken that oratorical accent does not degenerate into egotistical mannerism.

ECCLESIASTICAL ACCENT.*

"In Plain-song, the term 'accent' or *accentus ecclesiasticus* was used to designate that system of movement of the voice, by learning the principles of which (*modus legendi choraliter*) a chanter could read collects, epistles, gospels, etc., from an unnoted book. Hence it resolved itself into a series of rules relating to the inflexions or intonations of the voice on reaching a comma, semicolon, colon, full stop, and also a note of interrogation. But perfect uniformity is not to be found in these regulations regarding the *puncta*. According to its position in the sentence, or the interval covered by the movement of the voice, accent was said to be (1) *immutabilis*, (2) *medius*, (3) *gravis*, (4) *acutus*, (5) *moderatus*, (6) *interrogativus*, (7) *finalis*. The following are examples of these different species:—

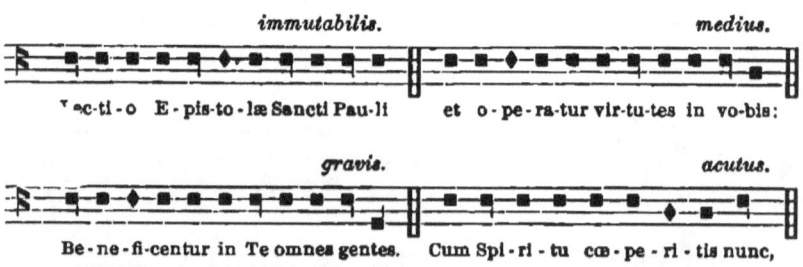

* Extracted from Stainer and Barrett's "Dictionary of Musical Terms," p. 4.

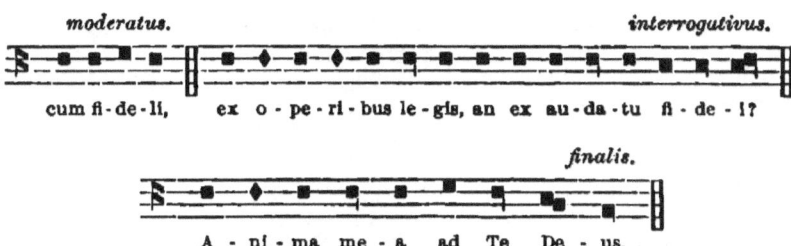

"But according to some authors, the epistle should be on monotone, except at a point of interrogation, *e.g.*:—

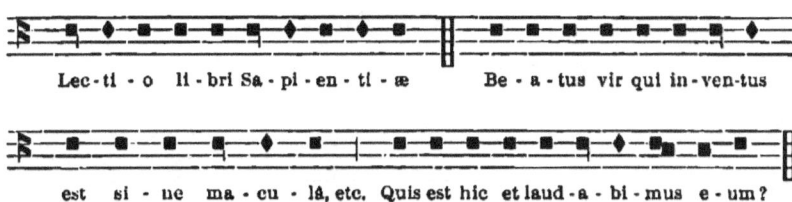

"But in some countries the epistle is chanted with the greatest elaboration, the note above the reciting note being introduced before the full stop, and the whole of an interrogative sentence being recited on a note below the *ut*. But as these uses differ not only in various places, but according to the Church seasons, an exhaustive account is impossible.

"In chanting the gospel, an *accentus medius* takes place at the fourth syllable from a full stop, or thereabouts, and also the *accentus interrogativus*:—

"In the chanting of collects, a fall from ut to la, or from fa to re takes place at a *punctum principale*, and from ut to si, or fa to mi once only at a *semipunctum*.

"The *accentus ecclesiasticus* of lections and prayers must not be confused with those inflexions which tradition assigns to other parts of the service, such as confessions, proper prefaces, and lections of the

Passion; all of which are to be found noted in authorized books. It should be remarked that the Belgian and French uses often differ much from that of the Romans, although uniformity in such things is without doubt desirable."

METRE.

"Metre is the rhythmical arrangement of syllables into verses, stanzas, strophes, etc.; poetical measure depending on number, quantity, and accent of syllables, rhythm, measure, verse." (WEBSTER.)

TABLE OF DIFFERENT METRES, AS APPLIED IN MUSIC.

DISSYLLABLES.

TROCHEE (— ⌣), long (heavy), short (light).

1. Simple.

2. Varied.

SPONDEE (— —), two long.

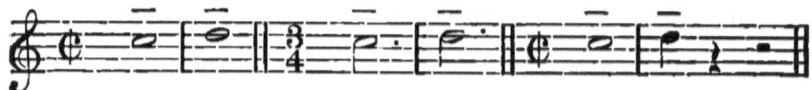

PYRRHIC (◡ ◡), two short.

Combined with — ◡ — it becomes an *Amphimacer*—

combined with — ◡ it becomes a Trochee—

and combined with — it becomes a Dactyl:—

TRISYLLABLES.

AMPHIBRACH (◡ — ◡), short (light), long (heavy), short (light).

MUSICAL FORMS.

CRETIC (— ᴗ —), long, short, long.

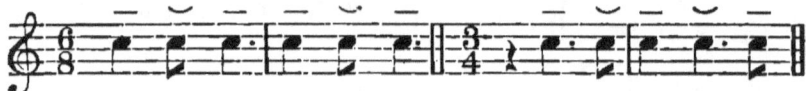

BEETHOVEN ("Eroica").

ANTIBACCHIC (ᴗ — —) one short, two long.

MOLOSSUS (— — —), three long.

SCHUBERT (Op. 163).

TRIBRACH (ᴗ ᴗ ᴗ), three short.

BEETHOVEN.

MENDELSSOHN.

In Beethoven's Seventh Symphony we find the following metres applied:—

HEAVY SPONDEES.

Introduction.

DACTYLS.

HEAVY DACTYLS AND SPONDEES.

DACTYLS AND TRIBRACHS.

HEAVY SPONDEES.

RHYTHM.

"Rhythm is the actual perception of the unity of a succession of moments in evolution." (APEL, *Metrik*, Leipzig, 1814-1816).—"The principle of rhythm is founded in the reciprocal effect, or in the condition of cause and effect." (HERRMANN, *Leipziger Musikzeitung*, vol. x, p. 289).—"The rhythm, which is in itself pleasing and beautiful, lies in the change of the succeeding parts of time, according to the law of exertion and rest, in which we have again to recognize a more forcible and a weaker exertion." (HOFFMAN).—"Rhythm is the united sum of different parts of time into a unit." (HAND, *Æsthetics of Music*).—"Rhythme c'est, dans sa définition la plus générale, la proportion qu'ont entre elles les parties d'un même tout; c'est en musique, la différence du mouvement qui résulte de la vitesse ou de la lenteur, de la longueur ou de la brèveté de temps." (ROUSSEAU, *Dictionnaire*, vol. ii, p. 242, Article "Rhythme.")—"Rhythm, a division of lines into short portions by a regular succession of *arses* and *theses*, or percussions and remissions of voice on words or syllables; the harmonious flow of vocal sounds. In the widest sense, a dividing of time into short portions by a regular succession of motions, impulses, sounds, etc., producing an agreeable effect, as in music, the dance, or the like." (WEBSTER).—"Rhythm, movement in musical time, or the periodical recurrence of accent; the measured beat which marks the character and expression of music." (MOORE).

We recognize in music three kinds of time-measure and order—first, *time*, the grouping of a succession of portions by the accent (see

Accent); the position of the principal notes of a melody as metrical heavy notes, that of the secondary notes as metrical light ones; secondly, we recognize further the *movement* (*tempo*), the relative degree of quickness of a piece; thirdly, the *rhythm*, under which head we again understand two separate things—(*a*) the joining of similar or different metrical feet into various figures: the sections of these figures are with regard to weight of time accented or unaccented, with regard to length of time they are either long or short, of higher or lower degree; through the bar (measure) and bar-accent they are collected into firmly united perceptible groups and time pictures. In this sense, each motive (theme) which consists of several notes or of notes and rests, and which is divided by a cæsura, either in a firm or light manner, is a rhythm. (*b*) Furthermore, we understand rhythm as the forming of these smaller rhythms or time-pictures into larger forms (periods and groups of periods) according to the rule of symmetry and proportion, the relation of the single melodious parts of a period to one another with regard to the nature of the division of time, the proportion of the first to the second part, the relation of each single part to the whole, and the proportions of movement of the single periods within the entire group of periods.

The rhythmical cæsuras, and sections of the period, as well as of the whole piece, result in firm and decided forms as comprehensible and satisfactory to our ear, just as the sight of a symmetrical and well-ordered structure affords pleasure to our eye. The development of one part out of another, the orderly grouping of the various periods, the support which one part receives through the other, indeed the systematic organic growth of the whole, regulated as it is by the rhythmical order, of which the human intelligence and feeling perceives, intuitively, the absolute necessity—all this contributes to the possibility of surveying and conceiving many single parts as constituting a whole.

The rhythmical construction of a musical piece cannot be definitely fixed according to a pattern or an arbitrary rule. The law that has to be obeyed does not restrict freedom of fancy and feeling; *variety* is necessary as well as *unity*. Rhythm is, indeed, the outward manifestation of the inner life; and the more harmonious, flowing, and rounded the inner movement is found, the more comprehensive, intelligible, and satisfactory will be the outward form.

The order and symmetry of rhythmical movement must never be stiff or too often repeated, as this would result in monotony: combined with *order* there must always be *freedom*. Rhythm may well be compared to the pulsation of the blood in the human frame; and just as such pulsation is accelerated or retarded by the emotions of the soul, so must the rhythmical life and expression change according to the character that it is the office of music to represent. Although rhythm will heighten the beauty of a melody, it can, even when used with the greatest cleverness, never succeed in ennobling vulgarity or triviality in music. In Greek and Latin poetry rhythm was developed and elaborated in the most artistic manner, and was employed as an exceedingly valuable means of strengthening and characterizing expression. But neither in music nor in poetry must rhythm be made the principal object, for it can never supply the place of inventive genius. Rhythm may be described as the art of the versifier—necessary, but yet only supplementary, to the genius of the poet.

[Musical notation examples labeled:]
RHYTHM OF SIX BARS.
RHYTHM OF EIGHT BARS.
RHYTHM OF FOUR BARS.
RHYTHM OF FOUR BARS. / HALF RHYTHM.
RHYTHM OF THREE BARS. / RHYTHM OF THREE BARS.
RHYTHM OF FOUR BARS. / RHYTHM OF FOUR BARS.

LITERATURE.—Young (Walter), "An Essay on Rhythmical Measures," "Transactions of the Royal Society of Edinburgh, 1790," vol. III, pt. i, pp. 55-110. Hermann (Gottfried), "Handbuch der Metrik;" Leipzig, 1799. Apel (Friedr. A. F.), "Metrik," 1814-1816. Baini (Giuseppe), "Saggio sopra l'identità de' ritmi musicale e poetico;" Firenze, 1820. Hauptman (M.), "Die Natur der Harmonik und Metrik;" Leipzig, 1873.

STYLE.

(Lat. *stilus*; Ital. *stile*.)

In creating a work of art the composer is subjected to certain rules of formal construction and of expression, rules which have their foundation in the nature of the art itself, and which, when applied, are influenced more or less by the subject which has to be represented.

The complete work of art must reveal itself in ideal beauty and purity, and will at all times be founded on truth of character and gracefulness of form.* The chief divisions of style in music, as indeed in poetry, are the epic, lyric, and dramatic style. In the epic style, the description is most prominent; feeling and representation are founded on an event, which has to be narrated in a poetical manner. The musical art cannot be said to possess such strictly epic works as we find in poetry; the epic style is in music merely an element, as exhibited in the oratorio, opera, cantata, in choruses, ballads, symphonies, or wherever the lyric expression assumes a broader and more pictorial character. In the lyric style the feeling is not objective, but subjective (personal); here expression and warmth of feeling are the chief ingredients of the music; but in so far as feeling is the chief promoter of music, the lyrical element must in some degree also influence the dramatic style. The dramatic style realizes, through visible action on the stage, the conception of events and actions; this visible action is performed by persons representing well-defined and positive characters. The dramatic style comprises the oratorio, opera, cantata; the chief forms of instrumental music, on the other hand, belong to the lyric style. We find, further, a difference between the secular and sacred style. The secular style, again, is subdivided into chamber and concert music, and into theatrical or dramatic style.

According to certain more prominent characteristic features which belong to works of art of different periods, musical history distinguishes periods as characterized by an artistic, grand, beautiful style, and so on. The period of the great school of the Netherlands—that of a Dufay, Ockenheim, and Josquin de Prés, until Willaert and Palestrina—is generally called the period of the *artistic* style in so far as the art of writing for several voices was particularly developed by the above-mentioned masters; the period of Palestrina and of the Roman school is known as that of the *grand* style; the period of the great Neapolitan masters as that of the *beautiful* style. From the national peculiarities of the different musical nations arose modifications of style, which we designate as the Italian, German, and French. From the different categories of the beautiful arise the tragic, grave, solemn, passionate, comic, cheerful, sympathetic, graceful, lofty style, etc., which, according to their nature, appear in works of arts of various kinds; and it need hardly be observed that the comic and passionate style must be excluded from sacred music, and can only appear in secular works.

Style varies also according to the material, which, as it were, is the channel of expression; for example, sometimes voices, at others, instruments, and again according to the manner in which the material is treated, that is, the connection and relation of tones to each other, by which the expression is variously influenced. Here there are two kinds of style, which are used sometimes separately and sometimes mingled with each other—namely, the *rigorous* and the *free* style. The rigorous style is founded upon the laws of vocal music and pure vocalism, and is known by a grave working out of the melody with a quiet progression and frequent ligaturas. We have here a stricter maintenance and working out of a principal subject, which must always be kept in view, and is transferred from one voice into another, whereby each voice obtains the character of a principal voice. This is the *polyphonic* method. (By polyphonism we understand multiplicity in sound; thus, musically, a composition in parts or contrapuntal composition.) It is

---

* Compare the Primer on the "Elements of the Beautiful in Music."

also distinguished by a frequent use of the prepared and resolved discords, by which the separate parts of the harmony are more closely intertwined, and by strict observance of the rule of rigorous writing. The highest forms of the rigorous style are the Canon and the Fugue, in which the arts of imitation and of counterpoint find especial application in the widest manner.

The *free* style, formerly also called the *elegant* style: here the movement of the melody and the treatment of the harmony with respect to the discords and the strict modulation of the keys are free, the voices are not all principal voices, for either there is only one principal melody prevailing throughout, which is merely accompanied by the other voices—(this is the homophonic style; homophony expresses sameness of sound or singing in unison in opposition to polyphony)—or if these other voices take part in the development of the principal melody or subject, this is not continuous; here a single principal melody does not rule so strictly, for it is varied in different ways by different subordinate subjects. The chorus can be treated either in the rigorous or in the free style according to circumstances; in the opera it is generally treated freely, although operatic choruses may be found worked out entirely in the contrapuntal or imitative manner, and the same may be said of arias and other forms.

Older designations of styles are the following:—

Stilus coraicus, the dance style of the minuets, gavottes, sarabandes, etc.

Stilus ecclesiasticus, especially adapted for church music.

Stilus familiaris, the simple style, used by Josquin de Prés in his so-called "Messe familiari."

Stilus hyporchematicus, the theatrical dance style, including certain lyrical songs accompanied by instruments and dance.

Stilus legatus, the connected legato style.

Stilus madrigalescus, in the style of a madrigal.

Stilus melismaticus, the ornamented style, with variations and elaborations of the melody.

Stilus moteticus, in the style of a motet.

Stilus fantasticus, to which fantasias, capriccios, toccatas, etc., belong.

Stilus recitativus, the dramatic style, especially adapted to portray the passions and emotions of the mind.

Stilus syllabicus, in which every syllable of the text has one note, as in recitatives.

Stilus symphoniacus, for instruments, with modifications for each separate instrument; quartets, symphonies, great overtures, etc., belong to this style.

FIGURE.

(Ital. *Figura*.)

Figure is a group of notes which results from the dissolution of melodious principal notes into diminished notes, or notes of a lesser value, on the same harmonious foundation. If the principal notes of a melody are dissolved into such figures, we call it a figured melody (*figuratus*); we accordingly speak also of a figured style, or manner. The *cantus figuralis*, although it may also occur as figured song, means more strictly, like the *cantus mensuralis*, the old manner used in the twelfth century, to sing notes of different value; whilst the *cantus planus* (choral melody) proceeded only in notes of the same value.

The principal notes may be figured in different manners—(a) by notes belonging to the same harmony, as—

(b) by using melodious discords—namely, suspensions, passing notes, and appoggiatura notes (*nota cambiata*, *Wechselnoten*) with the notes belonging to the principal harmony:—

* A remarkable example of these consecutive fifths is to be found in Bach's Toccata in D minor for the Organ.

Such figures were applied before the invention of the piano-forte, particularly in the compositions for keyed instruments—such as harpsichords, spinets, clavichords, also for the viol di gamba, and were called manners, graces, agréments, galanterien, etc. Our modern composers apply them much more sparingly. The student is advised to compare Emanuel Bach's "Versuch über die wahre Art das Clavier zu spielen;" Couperin and Champion de Chambonnière's "Tables d'agrèmens."

MELODY.

Melody is a succession of tones. The term "melody" is used (*a*) for tone succession, or connection of tones, as differing from *harmony*, a concord of tones, or the sounding of several tones together; (*b*) for a particular succession of tones, which succession is regulated by artistic and æsthetic rules and requirements.

(*a*) Every melody, even the simplest, must possess a certain, if ever so slight, connection between its single tones; this connection shows itself in (1) the proportion of the tones with regard to intervals; (2) their relation to the key and harmony; and (3) their vocal or singing quality. The intervals, as melodious parts of a succession of tones, must be considered from the point of lesser or greater difficulty for intonation :—

The augmented intervals, such as augmented fourths, fifths, etc., are not admissible in church music, as their characteristic expression lacks the quietness and evenness of the ordinary intervals. This rule is, however, only applicable to sacred music in the *alla cappella* style.

Succession of intervals.—An interval, in itself quite easy for singing, may become difficult by repetition; any one will find it easy to sing 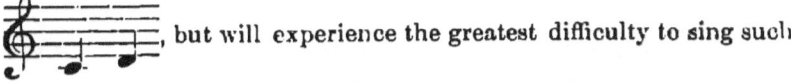, but will experience the greatest difficulty to sing such tones in succession as :—

Equally difficult and unvocal is  or a succession of thirds:—

Just as unvocal are all kinds of skips such as:—

All these remarks apply, however, to the melody as sung without the support of harmony; a judicious application of harmonious support will make them comparatively easy and even well sounding:—

The relation of the melody to the key and harmony ought to be always natural; the melody ought to move within the scale, and ought not to apply to notes foreign to the scale, as for instance:—

Foreign notes may, however, possess importance as belonging to a distinct harmony, and thereby occasioning a modulation—

or they are actually chromatic alterations of diatonic notes; such notes do not affect the harmony:—

(BEETHOVEN.)

The chief elements of a correct and natural progression of tones is best to be studied through counterpoint.

(b) *Melody*, in a special sense, is artistically constructed song, following the rules of melodious modulation, keeping in certain and definite relation to a key, proceeding in a rhythmical order, and exhibiting in tones a special feeling that has been aroused by certain impressions or passions The invention of a beautiful, singing, and expressive melody is one of surest signs of genius; but even the greatest genius will be anxious to purify, strengthen, and vary the melody by means of art and science; and in this respect no composer bestowed more pains and troubles on the perfection of his melodies than Beethoven did; his melodies are almost in every instance simple in point of progression, natural with regard to modulation, and highly interesting in point of rhythm. To cite only one example:—

It will be observed that each of the six bars contains a distinct rhythmical figure.

National melodies offer a delightful study for learning to construct natural and simple melodies. With respect to patriotic hymns or melodies intended to be sung by a great mass of people, it will be observed that they proceed mostly in the scale, or in the interval of a third, fourth, fifth or sixth, and that their modulation is of the simplest kind.

"GOD SAVE THE QUEEN."

"AUSTRIAN HYMN."

"RUSSIAN HYMN."

LITERATURE.—Nichelmann (Christoph.), 1717-1761, "Die Melodie nach ihrem Wesen, sowohi als nach ihren Eigenschaften." Reicha (Antoine), "Traité de Mélodie;" Paris, 1814. Santucci (Don Marco), "Dissertazione sulla Melodia;" Lucca, 1828.

THE PERIOD AND ITS CONSTRUCTION.

The *Period* is a form which is limited by a certain rhythmic, melodious, and harmonious order. The period can be in itself a small piece, or, combined with other periods, it may constitute a member of a longer piece. The order in which the different periods are united in a comprehensible and well regulated manner is called the construction of periods.

(1) Although the period must be clear and precise to be easily understood, the composer is not restricted to a stiff and rigorous scheme with regard to rule; but he may here, as in other parts of the composition, show his originality. We speak here of periods and their construction, appertaining to the domain of instrumental music, as vocal music is subject to the rules of poetry, which, however, are also governed by the same laws. A free and expanded movement of instrumental music could never be understood without a strict application of rules with regard to the construction of the period and of a well arranged systematic order, in which they succeed each other, and are, as it were, symmetrically distributed.

(2) As in the construction of the entire movement, so in the period, *unity* and at the same time *variety* are required. A movement which lacks variety becomes *monotonous;* it is deficient in development, it does not show different phases and features, which, spite of their variety, keep up a close connection with the principal idea. If the different periods were each the beginning of a new idea or motive, the result would be chaos, or might be compared to a pattern card.

(3) Taking the following simple periods of eight bars:—

34   MUSICAL FORMS.

in both examples we find a repetition of the same figure. In Ex. I. bars 5 and 6 are rhythmically the same as bars 1 and 2—in point of melody they are related to each other; in Ex. II. bars 1, 2, 5, and 6 contain the same figure, only on different intervals. In both periods we find certain figures, which form the chief material; these little figures, containing the germ of larger development, are called (4) *motives*. In Ex. II. the motives are more clear and precise than in Ex. I. With respect to the number of motives, a melody may possess very few, nay, it may even be restricted to a single one, and may yet be good; too many motives of different design would even endanger the clearness of the construction.

(5) In both periods we remark larger groups occasioned by the change and return of the motives; after every second bar we perceive the cæsura, which again determines the smaller groups called sections. The larger groups are divided into a preceding (first) and concluding (second) part. The preceding part generally contains the chief material of the motives of the period; the concluding part continues this material until it changes it in a freer manner towards the close.

(6) The order of modulation is the following: it begins and closes on the tonic (Ex. II.), the first part makes either a half cadence on the dominant or in a parallel key of the tonic. The second part begins either on the tonic or dominant, or in a related key.

(7) The period begins on the tonic and closes (in major) on the dominant (in minor), on the minor dominant, or in the parallel major key. The cadence of the first part follows either on the tonic or on the dominant, or in a related key, if the period begins on the dominant, passes and closes in the tonic, or in a related key. The close of the period on the dominant (or major parallel of the minor key) of course necessitates a repetition of the period itself with its close on the tonic, or a further elaboration.

(8) This simple period may undergo variations, either by alteration of its inner construction, or by an expansion or compression.

(a) Alteration of the inner construction—

Ex. III. BEETHOVEN.

(the second part is new and not developed from the first);

(b) The grouping and symmetry of bars is altered:—

Ex. IV.

This melody consists of eight bars, but in groups of twice three and a concluding group of two bars.

Expansion of the period is produced by (1) the imitation, or repetition of single motives:—

Ex. V.

(2) By the imitation of the first two bars, the period of four bars is expanded into one of six bars :—

Ex. VI.

By interpolation of the last two bars, a period of ten bars is produced.
(3) By the addition of a short appendix, formed out of one of the last motives of the period, a proceeding which strengthens and completes the expression :—

Ex. VII.

(4) By putting an introductory motive that leads into the actual period, which motive, however, is in itself an independent idea, and recurs in symmetrical order :—

Ex. VIII.

By compression, the first bar of the second part is wedged into the last bar of the first part, like (*b*) as compared with (*a*):—

Ex. IX.

This process was formerly called bar-stifling (Takterstickung):—

Ex. X.

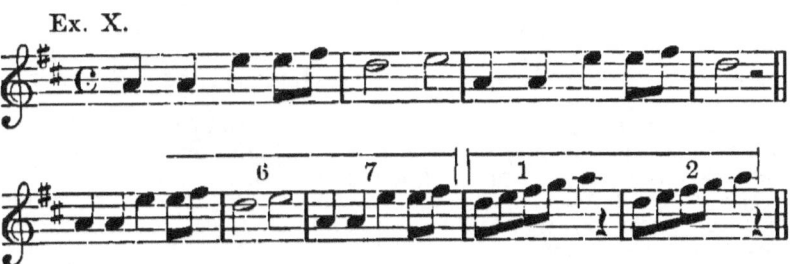

Compound periods result (1) from the repetition, with slight alterations of the same period, and (2) from a combination of different periods (group of periods). This latter method is shown in many beautiful instances in the sonatas and quartets of Haydn, Mozart, and Beethoven, excellent models with regard to symmetry, taste, and correct feeling. The most distinct and practical period is always that of eight bars. The best description of the period and its construction is to be found in the works of Dr. Bernhard Marx, "Die Lehre von der musikalischen Composition," vol. ii., and J. C. Lobe, "Compositionslehre."

THEMATIC WORK.

Thematic work is the *logical* development of the material of which the principal subject consists, and of which a piece is constructed into new periods, phases, features, etc., in such a manner that, notwithstanding alteration, the relation and connection of the new matter with the old is still recognizable. The means of thematic work are manifold. The following are the most important; *—

(1) The motive or principal subject is transformed *rhythmically*, whilst its harmony and melody remain undisturbed; in other words, the value of the notes is altered, the notes are multiplied or diminished, long notes are compressed into short ones, short notes expanded into long, the accentuation is altered, rhythmical changes (Rückungen), syncope, anticipations, etc., are introduced, the time is transformed from common into triple, ($\frac{2}{2}$ into $\frac{3}{2}$, $\frac{2}{4}$ into $\frac{3}{4}$, and so on), and the speed is altered by retardation or acceleration.

(2) Melodious alteration with unaltered harmony and rhythm, partial variations of the members constituting the melody, application of changes of direct movement into counter-movement, and *vice versa*; elaboration and ornamentation of parts of the principal melody, application of appoggiatura and passing notes, suspensions, melismas, or on the other hand the simplification of the melody by the withdrawal of all such ornaments. In these instances the connection with the principal air will be maintained by the rhythmical movement, inasmuch as through the elaboration of the melody the harmony will necessarily at times undergo a slight change.

(3) Alteration of harmony and melody, the rhythm being left intact; by the rhythm in this case is maintained the only resemblance with the principal motive.

(4) Alteration of the harmony; application of different successions of chords; transposition from major into minor key, and *vice versa*, which, of course, also affects the nature of the melody.

(5) Alteration of melody and rhythm; thus the thematic resemblance with the principal motive is vested in the harmony, which, of course, must consist of a very strongly pronounced and characteristic succession of chords.

(6) Alteration of the accompaniment; alteration of polyphonic style into a more simple one, and the reverse; variation of the supplementary accompanying parts in a characteristic manner.

(7) Variety of the contrapuntal treatment; imitative and canonic treatment; transposition of the motive into other parts; inversion by means of double counterpoint.

(8) Alteration of force and coloring of sound; change of the different degrees of force; augmentation or diminution of the instrumental masses; alteration of instrumentation.

(9) Alteration of register; transposition of the melody from the upper into the lower or middle register, and *vice versa*.

(10) Alteration of expression with regard to legato, staccato, portamento, etc.

---

* The limits of this book will not admit of any examples, but the student will do well to seek for the practical test of the present remarks in any of Beethoven's sonatas, quartets, or symphonies.

It will be seen that thematic work is founded on logical and economic principles. In seeking to draw all possible logical sequences from the principal subject chosen for work, the composer develops the very rich material he has in hand to work with; and, again, by economy in using this material, and by a wise distribution of it throughout the work itself, a never-ending variety and great and unfailing charm can be obtained. Moreover, the listener experiences a feeling of satisfaction, as the order, system, gradual appearance and disappearance of a melody, harmony, or rhythm, will be for him an object of curiosity, interest, and gratification. Thematic work is a musical maxim that is based on the laws of nature herself; it is identical with the law of organic production. This law demands that every product of the animal or vegetable world must develop itself according to a fixed economic order, and the nature of the germ contained within it. The instrumental works of Haydn, Mozart, Beethoven, and others of our best composers display a thoroughly logical and systematic development, which gradually unfolds itself from the *germ* or first idea to the point we technically call the *climax*. But just as we find that every animal or flower develops itself and receives its color and shape according to the given law, so do we detect in these great instrumental works that every part of the apparatus of the symphony, quartet, sonata, etc.—be it accompaniment, harmonization, imitation, rhythmical figure—is exactly suitable to the one subject treated; and thus it receives the stamp of perfection. The most ingenious writer would be unable to improve anything by alteration in a quartet, sonata, or symphony of Haydn, Mozart, or Beethoven; such a work could not be curtailed, lengthened or altered in the score; in short, every part of it is an absolute and logical necessity. Such is the nature of a piece in which the system and art of thematic work is carried out in its entirety; it is, in fact, the product of natural genius, of spontaneous inspiration, regulated and governed by the might of intelligence, suffused by science in its brightest aspect. Our illustrious masters, following out the rules and dictates of natural order, never forget that not only by intellectual and scientific means such glorious results might be achieved, but that they must at the same time be seconded and sustained by the feelings of a warm heart and the simplicity of a pure, unselfish, and genuine enthusiasm. Thematic work, in its best example, is therefore to be considered as the greatest triumph musical art can achieve.

Although we find germs of thematic works in Sebastian Bach's suites and partitas, sonatas and concertos—and it may be asserted that the strictest thematic work is to be found in the fugue the real inventors of thematic work—in our modern sense of the word are Haydn and Mozart, as shown in their string quartets and in some of their symphonies. Beethoven, however, brought this system to the greatest perfection. To name only three examples, we should cite the first movement of the Pastoral Symphony, the first movement of the Quartet in F, Op. 59, i., and the first movement of his grand Trio in B flat, Op. 97.

The student is strongly advised to examine and analyze the second parts of those movements. In most of the instruction books, thematic work was formerly called the development (Durchführung) of the principal motive or subject; it is only within the last twenty-five years that thematic work has been systematically and methodically treated by Dr. Bernhard Marx, and with still greater clearness and completeness by J. C. Lobe, in his "Lehrbuch der musikalischen Composition," vol. i. pp. 306-382. Very interesting material for study is also to be found in A. von Dommer's "Elemente der Musik," p. 158.

FORM WITH REGARD TO THE RELATION OF SEPARATE PARTS OF POLYPHONIC MUSIC.

COUNTERPOINT.

The term "Counterpoint," in its broadest sense, may be defined as "the art of adding one or more parts to a given melody (canto fermo);" in its more limited sense as "the art of harmonizing a theme by adding parts which shall be in themselves melodious." The terms, "subject," "melody," "canto fermo," and "theme," are synonymous.*

Counterpoint is simple or double. There are five species of simple counterpoint.

(1) When the added part is note against note of the subject:—

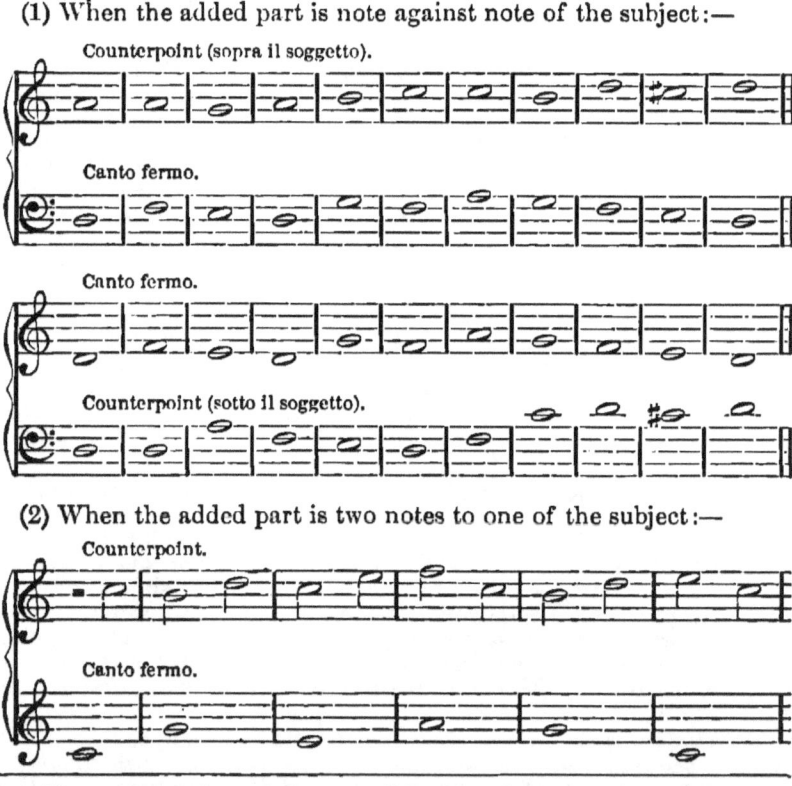

(2) When the added part is two notes to one of the subject:—

---

* About rules and regulations, see "Counterpoint" Primer, or Stainer and Barrett's "Dictionary of Musical Terms," pp. 112-119.

(3) When the added part is four notes to one of the subject:—

(4) When the added part is in syncopation to each note of the subject:—

(5) When the added part is free, or has a florid accompaniment to each note of the subject:—

DOUBLE COUNTERPOINT.

This has been well described as a kind of artificial composition, where the parts are inverted in such a manner that the uppermost becomes the lowermost, and *vice versa*, or in other words, the art of making melodies grammatically convertible at certain intervals.

If the melodies are interchanged at the interval of an octave, the double counterpoint is said to be at the octave; but if the inverted melody is transposed one note, the other melody remaining untransposed, the double counterpoint is said to be at the ninth, and so on.

The following table shows the effects of the inversion:—

		Free.	To be prepared and afterwards dissolved.
Double Counterpoint at the Octave	$\left\{\begin{array}{l}1,2,3,4,\\8,7,6,5.\end{array}\right\}$	1, 3, 6, 8.	2, 4, 7,
Do. do. Ninth	$\left\{\begin{array}{l}1,2,3,4,5,\\9,8,7,6,5.\end{array}\right\}$		
Do. do. Tenth	$\left\{\begin{array}{l}1,2,3,4,5,\\10,9,8,7,6.\end{array}\right\}$	1, 3, 5, 6, 8, 10.	2, 4, 7, 9.
Do. do. Eleventh	$\left\{\begin{array}{l}1,2,3,4,5,6,\\11,10,9,8,7,6,\end{array}\right\}$	6.	Discords of upper part: 11, 10, 9, 7, 4. Discords of lower part: 1, 2, 3, 4, 5, 8.
Do. do. Twelfth	$\left\{\begin{array}{l}1,2,3,4,5,6,\\12,11,10,9,8,7.\end{array}\right\}$	1, 3, 5, 8, 10, 12.	Discords of upper part: 11, 9, 7. Discords of lower part: 2, 4, 6.

(Musical notation: example showing inversion at the Ninth, with "Inverted into the Ninth." labeled below.)

The remaining double counterpoints at the 13th, 14th, 7th, 6th, 5th, 4th, and 3d, may be treated in a similar manner.

LITERATURE.—Marpurg (F. W.), New edition, revised and supplemented by S. Sechter; Vienna: Spina and Co. Martini (G. P.), Bologna, 1775. Sala (N.); Napoli, 1794. Morigi (A.), 1816; Leipzig: Breitkopf and Härtel. Fétis (F. J.), "Traité du Contrepoint;" Paris, 1825. Weber (Gottfried), 1831; Mayence: Schott. Cherubini (L.); London: Novello. Lobe (J. C.); Leipzig: Breitkopf and Härtel. Marx (Bernhard); Leipzig: Breitkopf and Härtel. Richter (E. F.); Leipzig: Breitkopf and Härtel. Novello, Ewer and Co.'s Primer. Sechter (Simon); Leipzig: Breitkopf and Härtel.

FUGUE.*

A Fugue (from the Italian *fuga*, "flight") is a composition written in the strictest style; in which a subject, being introduced by one part, is repeated and imitated by the other parts in succession, according to certain laws. The fugue in its simplest form is thus described by the German composer Fux, in his "Gradus ad Parnassum:"

---

* For a more detailed account than is possible in this work, see the Primer on "Fugue."

"First choose a subject suitable to the key you intend to compose in, and write down your part in that part wherewith you intend to begin. This done, and having first examined your subject, to see that it be conformable to your key, repeat the same notes in the second part, either in the fourth or fifth; and while the second part imitates the first wherewith you have begun, put such notes in the first part as will agree with your imitating part, according to the directions given in the figurative or florid counterpoint; and after having continued your melody for some bars, regulate the parts thus that the first cadence may be made on the fifth of the key. Then resume your subject mostly in the same part you have begun with, but by another interval, after having first put a rest of a whole or half bar, which, however, may be omitted in case there should be a great skip instead of it. After this endeavor to bring in your second part, after some rest, and that before the first part draws to a conclusion, and having carried on your subject a little longer, make your second cadence in the third of the key. Lastly, introduce your subject again in either part, and contrive it so that one part may imitate the other sooner than at first, and if possible after the first bar, whereupon both parts are to be united, and the fugue finished by a final cadence."

The following are the various forms of the fugue: *Fuga authentica*, a fugue in which the notes of the subject proceed upwards;—*Fuga a due o trè soggetti*, a fugue with two or three subjects;—*Fuga recta* or *composita*, a fugue where the subject proceeds by tones;—*Fuga contraria*, or *per motum contrarium*, in which the answer or imitation is already from the beginning in the inverted style; *Fuga doppia*, or double fugue;—*Fuga homophona*, in which the answer and imitation of the subject are in unison. The *Fuga impropria* or *irregularis* does not follow the strict rules. In the *Fuga incomposita* the subject proceeds by jerks. The *Fuga libera, soluta*, or *sciolta*, has free episodes or interpolated phrases. The *Fuga obbligata* unfolds itself according to absolute and logical rules. In the *Fuga per augmentationem* the imitation shows itself in augmentation; that is, if the subject is written in quavers, the first imitation is in crotchets, the second in minims, and so on. The *Fuga per diminutionem* follows this example in the opposite way.

Besides these, however, there are various other forms of fugues. No great oratorio or sacred work has yet been written, in which the composer was not anxious to provide a good fugue. The fugue is a kind of guarantee and importance given to the work, a testimony of legitimacy and genuineness, without which the work could not appear complete and perfect in the judgment of connoisseurs. All the rules accepted for instrumental fugues apply equally to vocal fugues. It is a matter of course that, owing to the more simple means and resources of the voice, the vocal fugue can never be so varied, brilliant, or complicated as one intended for instruments. Every composer of note, whether of old or modern times, has written fugues; but no composer has ever been able in this branch of our art to approach Sebastian Bach, whose Forty-eight Fugues and other numerous organ and choral fugues are monuments of constructive genius. He understood how to unravel all the scientific and artistic mysteries, to throw life, fluency, grace, and charm into his fugues, and he alone was able to present an almost unceasing variety of subjects, while he possessed inexhaustible means of enriching and enhancing the beauty and power of his themes.

FUGA A 3 VOCI.

GIACOMO ANTONIO PERTI (1656–1747).

CANON.

A *Canon* (from the Greek word meaning *rule*) is a musical composition, in which the voices begin one after another, at regular intervals, successively taking up the same subject; as each voice finishes, it commences anew, thus forming a continuous movement.

The canon was formerly also called *fuga canonica, legata, inconsequenza, integra, totalis*. The canon is a particular contrapuntal form. The point for starting the voice that succeeds the principal or initiating voice is not restricted to a fixed rule; and in the same way the choice of the interval in which the succeeding part begins is left to the composer's choice; thus we have *canons in the second* (Ex. III.), *third, fourth*, and so on; the composer must, however, adhere strictly to a rigorous and exact imitation of the principal or initiating voice. An exception to this rule is found in the so-called *free* canon, in which major intervals may be imitated by minor intervals, and *vice versa;* another exception is the so-called *false* or *mock (Schein) canon*, generally used in instrumental compositions (symphonies) and in operas; this kind of canon is called *canone sciolto*. According to the manner in which the close of the different parts is indicated, the canon is called *infinite (canon infinitus* or *perpetuus)* (Ex. I.), or *finite (canon finitus)*. In the first instance, each part begins again after the sentence is finished; in the second, each part is silent after having completed the sentence. In the *mixed canon (polymorphus)* (Ex. VII.), the second part follows the first part; for example in the fifth, whilst the third part can follow in another interval. The *circular canon (canon per tonos)* is produced by each part that begins occasioning a modulation, which method is repeated as many times as necessary to return to the starting or principal key. The *canon cancrizans* (Ex. VIII.) is a canon by retrogression; a canon practically consisting of two parts in double counterpoint, that is, parts which are grammatically interchangeable, so constructed that they may read actually backwards, hence probably, the derivation of cancrizans, walking backward like a crab. *Canon in augmentation* (Ex. VIII.) or *diminution* (Ex. IX.). In this, the succeeding part appears in notes of double or half the value of the initiating or principal part. The *double canon (canon duplex)* (Ex. X.), is the union of two separate canons. Other kinds of canons are: *canon enigmaticus*, the riddle canon, in which the difficulty is to find the proper place to start the succeeding part (every canon in which the place for commencing each succeeding part is not indicated may be regarded as a riddle canon); *canone al sospiro*, in which the parts follow each other closely, after a minim or a crotchet rest; the *canon in epidiapente*, in the upper dominant; in *epidiatessaron*, in the upper fourth; in *hypodiapason*, in the lower octave; in *hypodiatessaron*, in the lower fourth; *per arsin et thesin*, in mixed time. If the different parts of the canon are written out in full, in score (Ex. I.), it is called an *open canon (canone apertus)*; if, however, only the principal part is written out, and the number of parts (à, 2, 3, 4, etc.), and their respective entrances are marked by the sign $, the canon is called *a closed one (canon clausus, canone in corpo)* (Ex. II.). A few short examples will best show the different construction of canons.

MUSICAL FORMS.

CANON INFINITUS.

The parts written out (Canon apertus).

Ex. I. RAMEAU.

THE SAME CANON AS CANON CLAUSUS, CANONE IN CORPO:

Ex. II.

FORM IN MUSIC. 49

ANOTHER EXAMPLE FOR SIX PARTS.

KIRNBERGER.

CANON IN THE SECOND.

Ex. III.

CANON IN THE LOWER SEVENTH.

Ex. IV.

CANON IN THE UPPER THIRD (MEDIANT).

Ex. V.

ANDRE.

CANON POLYMORPHUS (MIXED).   SEB. BACH.

FORM IN MUSIC.

CANON CANCRIZANS.

Ex. VIII. ANDRE.

CANON IN AUGMENTATIONEM.

The second part (risposta) imitates the first part (proposta) in augmentation and in contrary motion.

Ex. IX. KIRNBERGER.
(1st part.)
Augmentatio.

(To make this example appear in the diminution, one has only to begin at †.)

DOUBLE CANON (CANON DUPLEX).

Ex. X.   Fux.

The above (Ex. X.) might also be called a Canon 4 in 2 because there are *four* parts having *two* distinct subjects. On the same principle Ex. I. shows a Canon 3 in 1 because there are three parts having one subject; Ex. III., IV., V. show Canons 2 in 1; Ex. VI. a Canon 4 in 1; the *first* number always showing the number of *parts;* the *second*, the number of *subjects.*

LITERATURE.—J. M. Bononcini, " Musicus practicus;" Stuttgart, 1701. Marpurg, "Abhandlung von der Fuge" (new edition, by S. Sechter); Vienna: Spina. Kirnberger, " Kunst des reinen Satzes;" Berlin, 1777. Albrechtsberger, "Anweisung zur Composition," p. 380; Vienna, 1829. Cherubini, " Cours de Contrepoint," p. 75. Anton (André); Offenbach, 1838. J. C. Lobe, " Lehrbuch der Composition," vol. iii.; Leipzig, 1860. S. W. Dehn, " Lehre vom Contrapunkt, Canon;" Berlin, 1859. Richter, " Lehrbuch der Fuge;" Leipzig, 1859. Bellermann (Th.), " Der Contrapunkt," etc., p. 285; Berlin, 1862.

VOCAL MUSIC.

SACRED FORMS.

ANTIPHONY.

IN the ancient Church of the Jews there was an alternation of song, one singer being answered by another or by a chorus in response, as in the Song of Moses and the Children of Israel, and of Miriam the Prophetess and all the women, with timbrels and with dances, after the passage of the Red Sea. This same alternation of song is to be traced in other notices of the Hebrew music throughout their history, as *e.g.* in I Samuel xviii. 7, "the women *answered one another* as they played." It was no doubt used at the first consecration of the Temple and its subsequent restorations, and in the daily Morning and Evening Sacrifices, at all of which a choral worship of the highest possible grandeur of vocal and instrumental music was celebrated. In the rebuilding of the Temple recorded by Ezra (iii. 10, 11) the choral arrangements were newly set on foot, " And they sang together *by course.* . . . And all the peple shouted with a great shout, when they praised the Lord." In Nehemiah xii. 24 the chief of the Levites are spoken of as having "their brethren *over against them*, to praise and to give thanks according to the commandment of David the man of God, ward *over against* ward." And at the dedication of the restored walls of Jerusalem the great procession of princes, priests, and Levites was divided into two companies, headed by "them that gave thanks," one going up from " the fountain-gate," " above the house of David, even unto the water-gate eastward;" and the other passing "*over against* them," above the old gate and other towers, stood still in the prison-gate. "And the singers sang loud, with Jezrahiah their overseer. . . . The wives also and the children rejoiced; so that the joy of Jerusalem was heard even afar off."

We know from Josephus that this choral worship, thus renewed after the Babylonish captivity, was continued in the Temple at Jerusalem until the final destruction of the holy city. We also learn from a treatise "On the Contemplative Life," by Philo Judæus, a Platonic philosopher of Alexandria (about A.D. 50), that the Jewish sect of the Therapeutæ, in their social worship, were in the habit of singing, in a similarly antiphonal manner, after supper: first in two choirs, one of men and another of women, each with a leader of superior skill and power of command, in the midst of the supper-room, hymns to the honor of God, composed in various metres and kinds of song. Afterwards, transported by their exercises both in processions and stations, by gesture and exultation, and a divine ecstasy, both choirs, the men and the women, joined together (as the Bacchantes used to do) in one choir, inebriated as it were in their pious rapture with pure draughts of the divine love, after the manner of their forefathers' rejoicings at their deliverance on the shores of the Red Sea. Thus they blended their deep and high voices in most sweet accord, and in pious, high-strained devotion they hailed the rising sun, and, with hands outstretched to heaven, prayed for a happy day, for the knowledge of the truth, and for clear mental vision. And thus ending their devotion, they each retired to their religious houses to work out and cultivate their accustomed philosophy.

The sacred song of the first Christians would necessarily partake largely of the characteristics of their national music, and, like other elements of divine worship, would naturally partake of such Templar peculiarities as were not, in the nature of things, mere shadows of a better dispensation. Neither prayer nor praise, nor vocal and instrumental music, were of the essence of the transitory rites of the Levitical dispensation; they were rather a foretaste of the celestial worship of Jerusalem above, and as such to be retained in the Christian, as they had originated in the Jewish Church. History confirms this supposition. From the first, Christian worship was antiphonal. Pliny the younger, Governor of Pontus and Bithynia, A.D. 110-111, stated in his letter to the Emperor Trajan, that the Christians affirmed that it was their practice to sing a hymn *by turns* to Christ as God; "carmen Christo quasi Deo dicere secum invicem." Socrates, in his "Ecclesiastical History," tells of Ignatius, Bishop of Antioch, who had conversed with the apostles, setting this antiphonal worship in order, and of his having had a vision of the angels thus adoring the Holy Trinity; and, as Hooker writes, "one which must be with us of greater authority," Isaiah, saw the Lord on a high throne; the Seraphim stood upon it, "*one cried unto another*, and said, Holy, holy, holy." The Psalms were the principal subject-matter of this antiphonal singing, and in St. Basil's time (A.D. 371) the custom was universal throughout the Eastern Churches of Egypt, Lybia, Thebes, Palestine—Arabians, Phœnicians, Syrians, Mesopotamians, and of all that reverenced the custom of singing psalms together; and he adds that "in this holy exercise the choir, being divided into two parts, they mutually answered each other" (ἀντιψάλλουσιν ἀλλήλοις). The word *antiphon* comes from the Greek ἀντί, "opposite," and φωνή, "a sound;" hence, in a general way, it expresses the alternate answering of one voice, or one set of voices, to another. But the term has, for upwards of thirteen centuries at least, been used specifically for the verse accompanying a psalm or group of psalms, taken sometimes from the psalm itself, sometimes from other sources, always suitable to the festival, or particular service in which it is used; and it serves to guide the worshipper to such an application of the ancient psalms as may transmute them into Christian hymns.

The music of the antiphon is more elaborate than the psalm-tone, being a regular melodic plain-song composition, with one or more notes to every syllable, and always ending on the final of its mode; thus, in any complete system of the ecclesiastical chant, the antiphon governs the psalm, and in a practical sense is a sort of burthen or refrain, sung as an introduction, and a final response to its accompanying psalm or psalms.*

HYMN.

The word Hymn (Greek ὕμνος; Lat. *hymnus*; Fr. and Ger. *Hymne*; Ital. *inno*) is, as St. Augustine says, "a song with the praise of God" ("Cantus est cum laude Dei"); and again, "Si laudas Deum, et non cantas, non dicis hymnum. Si cantas, et non laudas Deum, non dicis hymnum" (Augustin, in Psa. cxlviii). The hymn, as well as the Psalms and other spiritual songs, is coeval with Christianity itself. The New Testament not only commands their use, but contains some of the actual words sung by the first Christians. There are various historical allusions to the Church hymns in the first three centuries; and in the fourth they were specially composed and appointed to parts of the ritual by Bishop Hilary, of Poitiers, and by St. Ambrose. The music of hymns is as various as the prose and metrical forms of the words themselves. The celebrated "Te Deum" of St. Ambrose and St. Augustin, with its traditional Ambrosian melody, may serve as an example of prose hymns, or canticles; and the four sequences, still retained out of hundreds of others in the Roman Missal, together with the office hymns of the Breviary, are the best-known specimens of ancient metrical hymns.

The natural love of metre has from the earliest times exercised an immense influence upon the worship of mankind in general, and of the Christian Church in particular. Thus, notwithstanding the opposition to any new thing on the part of ecclesiastical bigots continually repeating itself, from the times when Sabellius and Marcellus incensed the Church of Neocesarea against St. Basil, as being an author of new devices in the service of God, a love of poetry and melody in various metres has handed down to our own days a vast collection of hymns, "the gradual accumulation of centuries; the offerings of different epochs, of different countries, of different minds, to the same treasury of the church."

At the era of the Reformation this taste ran into sad excess by the rejection of the prose forms of psalms, hymns and even of prayers themselves, in favor of metrical translations. Hymnody itself was nearly crushed out, both at home and abroad, under the weight of the Protestant versions of psalms and canticles, which not only banished the proper music of the old Catholic psalms and canticles,

---

* "Cum psalmodiis autem antiphonæ cantantur; secundum hujus enim melodiæ tonum Psalmodia intonatur ab uno unius chori, et a duobus choris alternatim cantatur, eaque absoluta, antiphona ab omnibus perfecte repetitur et communiter canitur."—PRÆTOR, *Synt.* i. 65.

causing them to be merely *read*, in slovenly antiphon of priest and people (or the vicarious parish clerk), but actually usurped the place of the ancient Christian hymns, and—as was erroneously believed by many conscientious English Churchmen—rendered it *illegal* to introduce any hymn, ancient or modern, instead of the old version of the Psalms by Sternhold and Hopkins, or the new by Tate and Brady. Religious fervor rebelled against such uncatholic restrictions and perversions; the Nonconformist Protestants, and the followers of Whitfield and Wesley, breaking away from the lugubrious strains of Genevan and Scotch Presbyterian (so-called) *psalmody*, introduced a more hearty and popular style of melody—not unfrequently, it must be said, vulgar and meretricious, both in principle and in form, but which has, among other collateral influences, happily superinduced in the more Catholic-minded among English Christians a return to the good old paths of ancient hymnody, and its plain-song melody; while modern hymns and modern tunes have been vastly improved in style by the revival of a more artistic and church-like taste consequent on the study of the purer forms of Church music.

AMBROSIAN HYMN

is a musical setting of the "Te Deum" in plain-song, thus called because the words are ascribed to Bishop Ambrosius of Milan. According to tradition this hymn was first sung by Ambrosius whilst christening St. Augustine, A.D. 386, and it is further stated that both Ambrosius and Augustine were inspired with the tune at the same time; but subsequent researches have shown that the hymn-tune is originally an oriental one, which was received by the Latin Church from the Greek Church.*

ANTHEM.

The word itself is said by some authors to be derived from ant-hymn, a kind of antiphony. According to H. Ch. Koch ("Musikalisches Lexicon"), and Mattheson ("Ehrenpforte") "anthem" was at first synonymous with "antiphony." Byrd, Tallis, and other of our earliest post-Reformation composers wrote anthems in the style of motets. Purcell and others at the Restoration introduced solo anthems, as had Orlando Gibbons in Charles I's reign. Handel wrote anthems which may be called a mixture of a motet and a German sacred cantata. From the motet Handel's anthem derived the broadly planned and artistically worked-out choruses (the words taken from the Bible); from the cantata the anthem took the solo parts and the orchestral accompaniments (see Chrysander's "Life of Handel," vol. i. p. 459). Another definition of the anthem is: "Anthem, a composition for voices, with or without organ or other instrumental accompaniments, enjoined by the ritual of the Anglican Church to be sung at morning and evening service, 'in choirs or places where they sing.'" It is an ornament of the service reserved for the choir, in which the congregation takes no part.

---

* See Rambach, "Anthologie christlicher Kirchengesänge," i. p. 91; Fortlage. "Gesänge christlicher Vorzeit," p. 367.

MOTET.

(Ital. *Motetto,* also *Moteta, Motecta, Muteta, Modeta.*)

The last species of the hymn we have to notice is the Motet. Opinions differ as to the origin of the word motet. The great German historian of music, Winterfeld, a high authority in matters of sacred music, derives the word motet from the French *mot,* or "word," from the fact that the text of a motet must always be a verse from the Bible. Other scholars think that it comes from *motus* and *movere,* "to move," inasmuch as the style of the motet is *livelier* and more *brisk* than that of other religious music; again it has been asserted that in *mutare,* "to change," the real origin of the word is to be sought, as the motet includes so many different ways of characteristic expression. The first motets were constructed on a *cantus firmus,* or plain-chant, which was taken from the Gregorian chant. From Bach, however, the motet received a much freer expression. That great master abandoned to some extent the *cantus firmus* and substituted for it the Protestant choral. In the Roman Mass a motet may be sung during the offertory.

MASS.

The Latin word is *missa*; the Italian *messa*; the French and German, *Messe.* All may be interpreted as meaning *Missa est,* "it is pronounced." The Mass comprises three parts: 1. The Offertorium, or Offertory; 2. The Benediction, or Blessing; 3. The Sumption, or Reception. These three parts respectively contain the following distinct pieces: the Kyrie Eleison, the Gloria, the Credo, the Sanctus, the Benedictus, and finally the Agnus Dei, with the additional "Dona nobis pacem." According to the number and rank of the officiating priests, the accompanying solemnity of ceremonial, and the co-operation of a choir, the Mass is called a High or Solemn Mass, or a Low Mass. It may safely be asserted that almost every composer of eminence wrote Masses; and if a complete list of these compositions were made, the number would without exaggeration amount to tens of thousands. Among the older composers the name of Giovanni P. Palestrina is especially identified with the Mass; and among the modern composers, the two Haydns (Joseph and Michael), Mozart, Cherubini, Beethoven, and Hummel.

The "Funeral Mass," which, as its name implies, is devoted to the memory of the dead, is called "Missa pro defunctis," or "Requiem," the latter title being an abridgment of the words of the Mass, "Requiem æternam dona eis;" or in English, "Rest eternal grant Thou to them." The order in which the service of the Requiem follows is:—

1. Requiem æternam, Kyrie Eleison. Reading of the prayer and epistle Tractus. 2. Dies iræ, dies illa. Prayer for eternal rest. 3. Domini Jesu Christe. 4. Sanctus, Benedictus. 5. Agnus Dei, Lux æterna. The two most celebrated compositions of this kind are by Mozart and Cherubini. Mozart's "Requiem" stands forth pre-eminent in our musical literature as something unapproachable by ordinary criticism, as a thing to be judged and measured only by its gigantic self. Sounds like those of the "Lacrymosa," and the thrilling chords with which the "Confutatis" closes, do not seem to belong to this

nether world; and indeed the illustrious composer, whose career was so sadly and prematurely closed, penned part of his "Requiem" actually on his deathbed; and while the shadows of death were closing around him he murmured passages of this his most beloved work.

The Mass, together with the Oratorio, forms the most important branch of sacred music; and, when we consider that it contains six distinct features or opportunities for expression, we cannot wonder at the many composers who have written in this form. One displayed his strength in the Benedictus, another in the Gloria; the Kyrie Eleison, with its supplementary Christe Eleison, was mostly used to exhibit skill in fugue-writing. Ultimately, especially in the south of Germany and Italy, the mode of writing Masses degenerated into a vulgar and frivolous style, devoid of all devotional and religious feeling; but on the other hand we have such masterpieces as the stupendous "Missa solemnis" of Beethoven, one of the greatest monuments of musical art. Before we proceed to the form of the Oratorio we have to mention some minor sacred forms, which have become celebrated through their respective composers.

INTROIT.

(Lat. *introitus;* Fr. *introit.*)

The commencement of the Liturgy proper—*i.e.* Holy Communion or Mass—is the Introit, of which there are authentic records from the beginning of the fifth century. Celestine I. ordered the Psalms of David; and St. Gregory the Great has set, in his famous "Antiphonary," one psalm to be sung antiphonally whilst the sacred ministers were proceeding from the sacristy and entering the presbyterium. The first Prayer Book of our Edward VI. also appoints a psalm for the introit for each Sunday in the year; and in a manner the place has been traditionally kept open for this beautiful introduction to the service by the use of a misplaced sanctus, a modern anthem, or a metrical hymn.

On Ferias (or ordinary weekdays) *one* chorister intones the antiphon; *two,* or *more,* on festivals, according to their solemnity. The entire choir after this commencement falls in, and finishes it; then the one or more choristers, as before mentioned, sing the half verse of the psalm, and, in its place, half of the Gloria Patri, the full choir responding with the remaining half.

The time for commencing the introit is when the celebrant has reached the altar-steps; and the music should be Gregorian, even when the other portions of the service are sung to harmonized music.

GRADUAL.

(Ger. *Stufen-* or *Staffelgesang.*)

We find the origin of the name of this form of song-writing in the word *gradus,* "steps." Whilst the gradual was sung by the chorus, the officiating priest either stood on the steps by the lectern, or ascended the steps of the altar, from which the Gospel was to be read. The gradual can be made the exponent of different kinds of sentiments, according as it is employed for the celebration of the respective holidays or feasts. The graduals used in the services of Christmas or of other joyful holidays have, as a coda, a hallelujah; and this again concludes with a so-called Jubilus on the vowel a, expressing, by means of certain florid passages, the joy of the congregation. The best modern graduals were written by Joseph and Michael Haydn, by Mozart, Cherubini, and Hummel. At present the gradual occupies in the Mass a position immediately after the Epistle.

OFFERTORY.

(Lat. and Ger. *Offertorium;* Fr. *offertoire;* Ital. *offertorio*.)

An anthem or hymn sung from the earliest times in the Liturgy, whilst the contributions of the faithful for the poor and other offerings were collected, and is still used while the celebrant is preparing to offer the oblations previous to the consecration of the elements.

The offertory properly consists of an extract from the Psalms or some other portion of Scripture. Like the introit, it is intoned by one, two, or three and four chanters, according to circumstances, and then continued to the end by the full choir.

In Paschal-time a hallelujah is added. If there be time a motet suited to the occasion may be sung after the offertory.

The expression of the offertory ought to be soft, devotional, and subdued.

STABAT MATER.

This work is one of the five sequences of the Latin Gradual, and, musically considered, a sacred cantata, which begins with the words "Stabat Mater dolorosa," and which describes the agony and suffering of the Holy Virgin standing at the Cross of the Saviour. The text has been attributed to various authors, among them Pope John XXII. and one of the Gregories; but generally the Franciscan friar Jacobus de Benedictus (commonly called Jacoponus) is credited with the composition of the somewhat quaint and uncouth verses. With regard to musical composition the "Stabat" for eight voices by Palestrina, that for two female voices by Pergolesi, that by Astorga, Joseph Haydn, and lastly that by Rossini (though this last is by no means strictly a sacred work) are the most renowned specimens of this kind of sacred song. When the Stabat is performed in the Roman Catholic Church it is used as a so-called "sequence" to be sung during the service of the "Seven Sufferings of the Virgin." The first lines of the five sequences retained in the Roman Catholic Church are: *Victimæ Paschali,* Easter; *Veni, Sancte Spiritus,* Pentecost; *Lauda Sion,* Corpus Christi; *Stabat Mater dolorosa,* Seven Dolors of B.V.M.; *Dies iræ,* a specialty of the Mass for the Dead.

MISERERE.

The *Miserere* is another celebrated composition; the "Miserere mei, Deus" (Lord, have mercy upon me) is in fact the fifty-first Psalm, and is daily sung in monasteries at midnight as a prayer to implore mercy for the coming day. When sung after midnight the service is called *Mattutino,* or in English, "Matins;" but when sung in the afternoon of Thursdays, Fridays, and Saturdays, during the Holy

Week it is called the Dark Service, or *Tenebræ*. The most famous Miserere is that by Allegri, sung during Easter Week by the choristers in the Sistine Chapel. When the Miserere begins, the pope and cardinals fall on their knees, and they remain in that position until its conclusion. It is well known that all copying of Allegri's composition was strictly forbidden. The work was for a long time the exclusive property of the papal choir; but this precaution was frustrated by the prodigious memory of Mozart, who at the age of fifteen heard Allegri's "Miserere" during his stay in Rome and noted it down on paper. There are two minor forms, the "Salva regina" and "Ave verum Corpus;" the former is founded on the words of Pietro di Compostella, and belongs to the antiphonies dedicated to the Feasts of the Holy Virgin; the latter is a short piece, mostly performed during the procession of the Corpus Christi.

LAMENTATIONS.

Lastly, we have to mention the "Lamentations," founded on the words of the prophet Jeremiah, and sung at night during Passion Week.

CANTICUM.

In English, "canticle," an ecclesiastical song of praise or a hymn. The three canticles from the New Testament—that of Mary, "My soul doth magnify the Lord;" that of Zacharias, "Blessed be the Lord God of Israel;" and that of Simeon, "Lord, now lettest Thou Thy servant"—were called *cantica majora* or *evangelica*, and were and are daily used in the Church service. The Old Testament contains seven smaller canticles (*minora*), distributed among the seven days of the week. The greater canticles are sung with their antiphonies in a slower and more solemn manner than the lesser canticles and ordinary psalmody.

MAGNIFICAT.

Canticum beatæ virginis (St. Luke i. 46-55). (See also Canticum.) One of three cantica majora or evangelica, beginning with the words "Magnificat anima mea Dominum" ("My soul doth magnify the Lord").

This hymn is used in the Roman Catholic as well as in the Protestant service, and has been set by many composers. (See Bona, "Psalmod." p. 525.) Among the most celebrated settings of the Magnificat may be named those of Erba, Sebastian Bach, Palestrina (Proske, A., vol. iii. p. 282), Lotti, Lassus (Proske, A., vol. iii. pp. 253-278), Pitoni (Lück, vol. ii. p. 220), Morales (Proske, A., vol. iii. p. 298), and Marenzio (Proske, A., vol. iii. p. 325).

LAUDA SION SALVATOREM.

The first sequence or service for the Corpus Christi, written by Thomas Aquinas, who wrote the liturgy for this feast in 1269, at the request of Pope Urban X. It is not known whether the very solemn melody was composed by the author of the words. (Noble examples of this style are Palestrina's Motet "Lauda Sion" for eight voices (1575), and Mendelssohn's similarly-named composition, written for Liege, 1845.)

LAUDES.

In the Roman Catholic Liturgy the term "*Laudes*" is applied to the Hallelujah which is sung between the Epistle and the Gospel; also, according to Walther, the last piece of the nocturnal service, for which the 148th Psalm and the two following were sung.

LAUDES EPISCOPI.

According to Koch's old Lexicon, Laudes Episcopi were old Gallic melodies, which were, up to the time of the French Revolution, sung by the canons in some French cathedrals before the epistle on the principal feast days.

LAUDI SPIRITUALI

were short hymns for four voices, composed by Animuccia and Palestrina for the services of prayer of Philippo Neri. These Laudi spirituali, sometimes alternating with a soliloquy, are in fact the modest beginning of the Oratorio.

ORATORIO.

The name *Oratorio* is derived from the "Oratory"—the sanctuary for prayer—in which the zealous Roman Priest St. Philippo Neri assembled his congregation. The first oratorios treated exclusively of the story of our Saviour's sufferings, and were by no means identical with the form, as elaborated and perfected by Handel or Mendelssohn; indeed the musical part of the ceremony might be called the subordinate one, in so far as the sermon, interpolated between the different choruses, occupied the longer time. The earliest specimens of the Italian Oratorio consisted of antiphonies, and more particularly of short choruses, which were called "Laudi spirituali." Neri's efforts to interest his congregation in this respect were most energetically seconded by Animuccia and Palestrina. The Oratorio, as it was performed in the oratory of Neri, could, however, not permanently fascinate his hearers; and as the invention of the Opera happened to take place at the same time in Florence, the tendency to introduce a certain dramatic element into the sacred form was soon apparent. The first dramatic oratorio, produced with the strange accessories of scenery and costume, was composed by Emilio del Cavaliere, and was called "L'Anima ed il Corpo" ("The Soul and the Body"). Later Italian composers—for instance Alessandro Scarlatti, and most particularly Carissimi—selected for treatment biblical subjects apart from the history of the Saviour; and the short but exceedingly beautiful oratorio "Jephtha" of Carissimi already exhibits all the chief component elements of the later oratorios of Handel. The master-mind of Handel could not fail to appreciate the wealth of intrinsic power and interest contained in the form of the Oratorio; and he infused still greater dramatic expression into it. He chose almost all his texts from the Old Testament, and concentrated the chief strength in the chorus. Thus we could call the Oratorio of Handel a kind of biblical drama; from this designation we shor'd, however, except his

"Messiah," which exhibits a more strictly lyrical expression.* Among the most celebrated Italian composers of oratorios are, Carissimi, Steffani, Alessandro Scarlatti, Hasse; and among the German composers we must name Schütz, Handel, Keyser, Telemann, Mattheson, Emanuel Bach, Graun, Spohr, Beethoven, and Mendelssohn. Though it had not the influence on the progress of music in general which was exercised by the Opera, the Oratorio occupies one of the chief places amongst musical forms; and the great perfection which choral-writing has achieved is, if not *entirely*, at least *greatly* due to the Oratorio.

LITERATURE.—Chrysander (Fr.), "Ueber das Oratorium;" Schwerin, 1853. Bitter (C. H.), Beiträge zur Geschichte des Oratoriums;" Berlin, 1872. Finck (G. W.), "Encyclopädie des gesammten musikalischen Wissenschaften," vol. v. pp. 259-268; Stuttgart, 1837. Winterfeld (C. G. A.), "Johannes Gabrieli und sein Zeitalter;" Berlin 1834, II. D. Jahn (Otto), "Ueber Mendelssohn's Paulus.'" "Gesammelte Aufsätze über Musik," pp. 13-20; Leipzig, 1866.

PASSION-MUSIC.

As a branch of the Oratorio we must mention the *Passion-music*. The Passion-music originated in the Mysteries or Passion-plays; and at a later period adapted itself to almost all the forms which the Oratorio had taken. The chief difference between the Passion-music and the Oratorio is first of all that the Passion-music necessarily treats of the sufferings and death of our Saviour—that the story is related in the words of one of the Evangelists—and that the so-called *imaginary* congregation takes a part in the action by singing chorals. As the choral is essentially an integral part of the Protestant service, it necessarily follows that Passion-music has been chiefly composed by Protestant and especially German masters; for it was in Germany that Protestantism first took root. The introduction of chorals in Mendelssohn's oratorio of "St. Paul" is an adaptation of Bach's method. The following quotation is of interest:—

---

* F. Naumann, in his interesting work "Deutsche Tondichter," makes the following remarks about Handel's oratorios: "Most nations possess some great epic poem, constructed more or less on the model of the 'Iliad' and the 'Odyssey.' Thus, the Germans have the 'Nibelungenlied,' the Italians 'La Divina Commedia,' the English 'Paradise Lost.' Among the epic personages of the Israel of old are Esther, Deborah, Athalia, Judas Maccabæus, Joseph, Joshua, Solomon, Jephtha, Saul, and Samson; and to celebrate these personages in lofty song was surely a noble task for a composer whose own nature and character were essentially heroic. Milton's genius soared to the contemplation of the highest truths vouchsafed to man, and so it was with Handel. Although we associate the word Oratorio, which generally designates a sacred composition, with the works of Handel, these works might more properly be termed 'musical epics,' for it was chiefly the heroic or epic form he found in his subject, which he represented so gloriously in his music. When, for instance, in his 'Judas Maccabæus,' the chorus shouts—

Lead on, lead on! Judah disdains the galling load of hostile chains,

it is decidedly a martial hero rather than a sacred religious personage who is invoked. In the oratorios of Handel the religious element forms merely the back-ground; one single oratorio we of course except from this observation, and this is the 'Messiah.' That Handel's oratorios are really treated as epic, not as religious pieces, will be abundantly proved by reference to his 'Alexander's Feast,' 'Acis and Galatea,' 'Belshazzar,' 'Hercules,' and 'Semele.'"

"From primitive times it was the custom of the Church to keep green the memory of the sacred history by a public recitation, on Palm Sunday and Good Friday, of those chapters in one or other of the Gospels which relate the circumstances of the Passion. To give dramatic force to the narration the several personages who speak in the course of it were represented by different individuals, whereas he who recites the story was, throughout, the same. Thus a letter of Mendelssohn recounts how, at Rome among the solemnities of Passion Week, in the Sistine Chapel, in 1831, the portion of St. John's Gospel was sung on Good Friday, when the part of the Evangelist was sustained by a tenor, the words belonging to Jesus were assigned to a bass, those of Peter, Pilate, and the Maid Servant were given by an alto, and those of the multitude—whether the disciples, the populace, or the priests—were sung by the chorus. These choral fragments are defined as Turbæ. The whole was chanted upon so-called Gregorian tones; and its Roman use in the same form and to the same music has been from time immemorial.

"It was a special design of Luther to retain, in the Reformed Church, this primitive usage of periodically reciting the story of the Passion. According to his desire the simple manner of its intonation in his own time, by two priests only, was early amplified, and a German version of the text was printed at Wittenburg, in 1573, with music for the recitation, and introductory and final choruses, which, like the Turbæ, are harmonized in four parts. A more elaborated composition appeared in 1588, the work of Bartholomäus Gese, in which the part of Jesus is always set for four voices, those of Peter and Pilate for three, those of the Maid Servants for two, and the Turbæ are written for five voices—a peculiar distribution, that would distinguish the several individualities, but little tend to the dramatic effect of the performance. Heinrich Schütz, one of the most distinguished musicians of his time, composed, shortly before the close of his very long life, music for the Passion, as related in each of the four Gospels. The advanced resources of the art are applied in each of these four works, especially in the elaboration of the chorals or hymn-tunes that constitute the final choruses. In 1672, the year of the death of Schütz, Johann Sebastiani produced a 'Passion,' in which, for the first time, the part of the Evangelist, or narrator, was set to original recitative, instead of to the old ecclesiastical plain-song, and in which, also for the first time, string instruments were employed, instead of the accompaniment being restricted to the organ.

"The great advance that had been made in dramatic music, at the beginning of the eighteenth century, which was especially manifest in Hamburg, induced there the extended development of art forms in the settings of the 'Passion.' So, in 1704, the voluminous Reinhard Keiser, who was then director of the opera in that city, brought out 'Der Blutige und Sterbende Jesus,' a work to the same purpose of relating the Gospel story, but peculiar in being set to an original poem instead of to the biblical text. In this first occurs the term 'soliloquia,' to define a species of cantata or intermixture of recitative and rhythmical movements, of which there are three specimens in the work, that consist of reflections, for a single voice, upon the principal incidents. Another composition by Keiser appeared in 1712, which also was set to an original poem, wherein, however, the scriptural order of the story was more strictly followed than in the preceding.

"The text of this work was by Brockes, a Hamburg poet, and it seems to have been highly esteemed, for it was set to music also by Handel, in 1717, by Telemann and by Mattheson, and some passages from it are introduced in St. John's version of the Passion, as set by Bach. Handel composed another work on the same subject, when but nineteen years old, during his sojourn in Hamburg in 1704, which, as well as the production of 1717, is interspersed with chorals after the manner of the early Lutheran Church, pursued also by Bach." *

LITERATURE.—Mosewius, "J. S. Bach's Matthäus-passion;" Berlin, 1852. Chrysander (Fr.), "Handel," vol. i. p. 38. Dommer (A. von), "Elemente der Musik," p. 353. Macfarren (G. A.), Preface to Seb. Bach's "Passion of St. Matthew;" London: Novello, Ewer and Co.

---

* Extracted from Sir G. A. MACFARREN's Preface to Sebastian Bach's music of the *Passion according to St. Matthew.*

CHORAL.

The *Choral* itself must rank as a strictly Protestant musical form. The choral is essentially a psalm-tune. Its origin may be traced as far back as the time of Gregory I.; but the modern choral, which we derive from Martin Luther, is quite distinct from those tunes used in the Roman Catholic Church. It was the endeavor of the great Reformer to incite the people to a more active participation in the religious service; therefore he chose the most popular national melodies, to which he wrote sacred words, mostly paraphrases of the Psalms. As it had been customary with earlier Italian composers to construct their fugues, canons, and other choruses on the foundation of the Ambrosian or Gregorian chant, so it became a habit with Sebastian Bach and his followers to build the most complicated works upon the foundation of a choral. Some of the most interesting specimens of this form of sacred song are to be found in Bach's St. Matthew Passion, in his "Christmas Oratorio," and in his numerous motets and cantatas.

It may be asserted that the choral owes its existence to the obstacles which the Roman Catholic clergy placed in the way of the Germans, whom they tried to prevent from singing their religious hymns in their native language. From time immemorial the Germans were used to sing their war-songs and ballads in their own language. The Roman Church, always an enemy to nationality, forbade with all its authority the use of the German language, and vainly tried to prevent the excellent monks Otfried from Weissenburg (in Alsace), Rutpert of St. Gallen, and Wather Labeo, another Swiss, from introducing German hymns into the Roman Catholic Liturgy. The tyranny of the Church of Rome went so far as to shut out the congregation from all active participation in the service, save from responding with a "Kyrie Eleison" and "Christe Eleison," whilst the singing of the Psalms and hymns were confided solely to the officiating clergy. This strange prohibition was maintained in such a ridiculous degree that during one single service the congregation had to repeat about three hundred times the "Kyrie Eleison." Such exaggeration could not result in anything but mere senseless noise; and at last permission was given for the translation of hymns with Latin words into German, on condition, however, that each verse of these songs was to finish with the "Kyrie Eleison." From this refrain originates the term "Leisen," given to hymns of this kind. It was not till the twelfth century, when the Crusades gave a stimulus to religious enthusiasm, that poets wrote sacred songs in Germany and adapted them to the tunes of the before-mentioned "Leisen." Thus the earliest popular sacred music had its origin among the Germans; and the people, forbidden to take part in the Church service in their native language, could not be prevented from singing their simple national hymns on solemn and festive occasions, like the annual pilgrimage to Rome, the Feast of Corpus Christi, during the annual memorial Feasts of Saints, or in time of general supplications for rain, for fine weather, etc. These national songs received great encouragement through the minstrels (Minnesänger), in as far as the songs of these poets, although generally secular, were received with universal favor, and obtained more than a transitory influence. Thus we find flourishing at that time "*Marienlieder*," or songs in honor of the Holy

Virgin; the songs of the *palmers* or *pilgrims;* the songs of the *boatmen* and the religious *war-songs*. Among the latter we may mention the song, sung by the German troops during the war of their Emperor Rodolph of Hapsburg, and Ottokar of Bohemia, in 1273. It begins thus:—

> Holy Mary, mother and maid,
> All our grief to thee be said.

Another well-known hymn was that sung during the festival of Whitsuntide:—

> And now to the Holy Ghost we pray
> To give us the right belief alway:
> That, as to our life's end, guard may be,
> And from all our woe may set us free.
> *Kyrie Eleison.*

This hymn was adapted by Luther, under the name "And now we pray to the Holy Ghost." Apart from the above-named instances of the use of religious songs in the "vulgar tongue" of the various worshippers, the *Waldenses* in France, and the *Heretics* of Germany, established the institution of secular psalm-singing as a specialty of their creed. That a similar movement occurred at a later period in England is shown by the epithet "psalmsingers," contemptuously applied by the cavaliers in Charles I.'s time to their jealous though fanatical foes.

The members of another religious sect, that of the *Flagellants*, which had declared itself independent of the Roman hierarchy, sang German religious songs and contributed largely to popularize this custom. But it was not till in the fifteenth century that regular German church songs were written, and generally accepted, and this most important fact we owe to Johann Huss, the Wickcliffe of Bohemia. Although the Council of Constanz forbade in 1415 the use of these songs, they had already taken too firm a hold in the people's hearts to be effectually prohibited, and after the time of Huss the community of *Bohemian* or *Moravian* brothers did everything in their power to improve these hymns and establish their use. Four hundred were collected by Bishop Lucas, and published in 1504. This is in reality the first hymn-book containing melodies set to native words. We come now to the question—from what materials were these songs collected? We find that they may be classed into four categories:—

1. German translations of Latin church hymns.
2. Half German and half Latin, or so-called *mixed* songs; a strange assortment written, almost as a pastime by the monks, and whimsically made up of dog-Latin and modern languages.
3. Original German songs for religious festivals, etc.
4. Paraphrases of German national and love songs.

Of this last class it may not be uninteresting to cite a few examples. Their boldness and their outspoken language would produce an almost repulsive impression of profanity, weighed by a modern standard; but in matters of history we must be tolerant and bear in mind that in those days many things were uttered in mere simplicity of heart, while in later times the humble and low origin of these songs was forgotten. In one case the secular song runs thus:—

> The dearest lover whom I have,
> Lies in the host his cellar.

Of this very outspoken sentiment appeared the following astounding contrafactum or paraphrase:—

> The dearest master that I have,
> Is bound by love to me.

Another song runs thus:—

> There was a man had lost his wife.

Contrafactum, in a sacred style:—

> There was a man had lost God's grace.

In the same manner is the well-known secular Journeyman's Song:—

Out of these vulgar, seemingly insignificant elements the Protestant choral arose. That such songs could not satisfy public feeling for any length of time, is evident; and we shall find that Luther's translation of the Bible did not only furnish the foundation for the High-German language, but also presented a model for the excellent church hymns, of which the Protestant Church of Germany can boast so great a number, and of which many have become popular in an English garb. Luther writes to his friend George Spalatin: "It is my intention to write German psalms for the people, after the example of the Prophets and the old Fathers of the Church. . . . . Therefore we are seeking poets everywhere. . . . . I would pray, however, that the new words be kept away from the court, that they may all be according to the capacity of the common people, *quite simple and vulgar, and yet come out in a clear and telling way, and that the meaning be given full plainly, and according to the spirit of the psalm.*" The suggestion of Luther met with almost universal approval, and his ideas soon received an artistic development. "The people sang themselves into enthusiasm for the new religion, and many who were hostile to the name of Luther were converted to his tenets by the irresistible charm of the simple and touching Protestant Church psalmody."

LITERATURE.—Schamelias (Johann Martin), "Evangelischer Lieder Commentarius;" Leipzig, 1737. Riederer (Johann Bartholomæus), "Abhandlung von Einführung des deutschen Gesanges," etc.; Nürnberg, 1759. Schobor (David Gottfried), "Beitrag zur Lieder-Historie," etc.; Leipzig, 1760. "Kurze Geschichte der deutschen Kirchenlieder," Coburg, 1775. Kocher (Conrad), "Die Tonkunst in der Kirche," etc.; Stuttgart, 1823. Böhmer (J. G.), "Ueber Kirchenmusik, etc., in der Eutonia," 1831, vol. v. pp. 25–43. Wolf (Johann), "Kurze Geschichte des deutschen Kirchengesanges;" Göttingen, 1815.

THE FIGURED CHORAL.

This is a contrapuntal elaboration of all or of the separate parts of the choral by means of melodiously moving figures; it can be arranged for song with or without orchestra or especially for the organ. The most simple application of it is generally used by the organist, in so far as he tries to introduce a certain figure (in the middle or upper parts) whilst the choral is being sung. We here give an example from Sebastian Bach:—

"HERZLICH THUT MICH VERLANGEN."

But the figured choral is also used as a kind of prelude, in so far as the organist takes the choral, afterwards to be sung by the congregation, for the cantus firmus, and elaborates it with all possible contrapuntal, melodious, and harmonious devices. In this art no one has excelled so much as Sebastian Bach, whose "Choral-Vorspiele" (Preludes) are marvellous instances of consummate mastery over all scientific rules; exhibiting a complete command of every combination recognized in the musical art. The student is advised to examine carefully the following chorals in Bach's arrangement:—Peters's edition, No. 23, vol. ii. pp. 201, 233, 235, 271, 280, 286 (from the "Christmas Oratorio"), 298, 319. C. von Winterfield, "Evangelische Kirchengesänge," vol. iii. pp. 172, 226, 230; Leipzig: Breitkopf and Härtel.

PSALMS (*psalmus, salmo*), PSALMODY (*psalmodia*).

The poems ascribed to King David were also introduced in the earliest times into Christian worship, and the people were never tired of singing them before and after their meals and of using them at their prayers. The manner of singing the Psalms is called *psalmody;* it is actually a medium between reciting and speaking, each psalm-tune is bound to a certain tonality. In its rhythmical expression it follows strictly the metre of the words, and marks the beginning of the verse merely by an upward or downward movement; whilst the voice keeps, during the beginning of the verse, on one tone only.

Ad te le - va - vi o - cu - los me - os. Qui ha - bi - tas in cœ - lis.

The psalm was preceded by an antiphony or was united with it, and was sung in the same tone; the end was the smaller doxology (*Doxologia parva*) "Gloria Patri," on whose final formula, "Seculorum amen," the voice was raised to real singing or to pneumas. The Psalms were sung in four different manners: (*a*) by a single voice; (*b*) by the whole congregation; (*c*) by the congregation divided into two parts and then sung like antiphonies; or (*d*) by one voice, with the chorus joining at the conclusion. Particular psalms are selected for certain solemnities and feast-days. The canticles (see Canticus) are also reckoned to the Psalms. In the German Protestant service the psalmody is still used by the officiating clergyman under the name of Collectengesang.

The Italian composers have written many psalms, and we possess in new editions very rich and well-selected collections. Among more modern Italian composers may be mentioned Benedetto Marcello, whose fifty psalm compositions appeared: in 1724 the first volume, "Estro Poetico Armonico: Parafrasi sopra li primi venticinque salmi;" in 1726–1727 the second volume, "Estro Poetico Armonico: Parafrasi sopra i secondi venticinque salmi."

Among the older German composers the Psalms of Heinrich Schütz ("Sagittarius") are most remarkable works; and among the modern composers the Psalms of Mendelssohn, 42d, 95th, 114th, with orchestral accompaniment, and the three Psalms (Op. 78) for eight voices, written for the Berlin Cathedral Choir, belong to the finest creations of that excellent master.

CONCERTO DA CHIESA.

The Church Concerto was introduced by Ludovico Viadana (1560–1625). The motets were in his time so overcrowded with all possible contrapuntal artifices that of the words scarcely anything could be heard; "it resulted in such a confusion and noise that one could not understand a single word much less a sentence" (Printz, "Histor. Beschreibung," p. 133). To do more justice to the words, Viadana adapted the monodies (song for one voice) and concertos. The expression, "Concert concertus" (see this form) was, however, already used before Viadana, not so much as the name of a special musical form, as for describing in general a composition in several parts. The most simple kind of his concertos Viadana composed for one voice, with an organ-continuo (figured bass); others he set for two, three or four voices, also with organ accompaniment. (Frankfurt, 1602, 100 songs; 1615 and 1625, 146 songs.) At a later time more instruments were used, the Concerto da Chiesa was composed *senza e con stromenti*. On the other hand it must not be supposed that Viadana's Concerto was anything like our modern concerto. These sacred concertos were short; all the parts were treated as principal or obbligato parts. The text was generally a verse of one of the Psalms or any other biblical sentence.

LITERATURE.—Clerc (Don Jacob de), "La science et la pratique du pleinchant, par un Réligieux de la Congrégation de St. Maur;" Paris, 1672. Martenius or Martène (Edmund) (1654-1739), "Traité de l'ancienne discipline de l'église dans la célébration de l'office divin;" Paris, 1719. Calvör (Caspar) (1650-1725), "De Musica ac sigillatim de ecclesiastica eoque spectantibus organis:" Leipzig, 1702. Pagi (Franciscus) (1654-1721), "Breviarium historico-chronologico-criticum," etc.; Antwerp, 1717. Scheibel (Gottfried Ephraim), "Die Geschichte der Kirchenmusik alter und neuer Zeiten;" Breslau, 1738. Pittono (Joh. Baptista), "Constitutiones pontificæ et Romanorum congregationum decisiones ad sacros ritus spectantes," etc.; Venezia, 1740. Gerbert von Hornau (Prince Martin) (1720-1793), "De Cantu et Musica sacra a prima ecclesiæ ætate usque ad præseus tempus," 1774. "Historical and Critical Essay on the Cathedral Music;" London, 1783. Vogler (Georg Joseph), "Ueber Choral und Kirchengesänge;" München, 1814. Hoffmann (Heinr.), "Geschichte des deutschen Kirchenliedes bis auf Luther's Zeit," Breslau, 1832. Häuser (Joh. Ernst), "Geschichte des christlichen Kirchengesanges und der Kirchenmusik," etc.; Leipzig, 1834. Olearius (Joh. Christoph.) (1611-1688), "Geistliche Singekunst" Leipzig, 1671. Kocher (Conrad), "Die Tonkunst in der Kirche," etc.; Stuttgart, 1823. Becker (Carl Ferdinand), "Sammlung von Chorälen aus dem 16ten und 17ten Jahrhundert;" Leipzig, 1831. Chrysander (Friedrich), "Ueber das Oratorium;" Schwerin, 1853. Winterfeld (C. von), "Der evangelische Kirchengesang;" Leipzig, 1843. Breitkopf and Härtel. Winterfeld (C. von), "Zur Geschichte heiliger Tonkunst;" Leipzig, 1850. Tucher (F. von), "Schatz des evangelischen Kirchengesanges;" Leipzig. Home (George), "The Antiquity, Use, and Excellence of Church Music;" London: Rivington, 1784. "Jour. Encyclop.," Mai, 1785, p. 166.

FORMS BELONGING TO SACRED AND SECULAR VOCAL MUSIC.

RECITATIVE.

(Ital. *Recitativo*.)

THE *Recitative* is a form of expression belonging to dramatic music, and occupying a position between declamation and actual singing. All singing is nothing else, or should be nothing else, but the effusion of an overflowing heart in sounds, in which the articulated sounds of speech adopt that passive modification of tone which we call the singing voice. If the state of feeling is a lasting one the expression of the music becomes also systematized—in fact it becomes a melody; in dramatic music it takes the form of an aria (see Aria), which represents the climax of the feeling. But where the feeling is merely awakening or gradually growing, or spasmodically appearing and disappearing, the musical expression cannot yet be a solid or firm one, and therefore the music seeks for a mode of expression which holds the balance between passionate language (declamation) and actual singing. This mode of expression is the recitative.

The recitative differs from ordinary declamation in the following particulars:—(1) The articulated spoken tone approximates to a certain degree to the tone that is sung; (2) by an order of succession of tones which admit of the assistance of harmony (this harmony may rest undisturbed for some time or modulate into other keys). From real song the recitative differs in the following points:—(1) The recitative is not bound to any particular or systematic time; the singer dwells only on words which even in speaking require a certain emphasis and accent; the other words succeed each other quickly, and it is not necessary to pay much attention to the special value of the notes; so long as a clear and intelligible pronunciation prevails the actual aim of the recitative with regard to time is satisfied and attained. In the oratorio and sacred cantata the recitative is generally sung in a more solemn and grave manner, but in the opera, and more particularly in the comic opera, it would be unbearable to listen to a recitative sung with a pathetic or grand expression. The recitative is brought within the frame of a bar only for this reason, that the sense of the words becomes clearer to the singer, and that the composer may, through the application of arsis and thesis (see Accent), show which words or syllables he desires to emphasize. The Italian and German composers always put the recitative in common time; some French composers, however, mix common with triple time, thus occasioning a good deal of confusion. (2) The recitative has no rhythmic symmetrical parts, only the cæsuræ of the text are observed, regardless of the symmetry of the melodious element; rests or pauses appear only where the words require them through an interpunctuation. (3) The recitative is purely syllabic; has not more tones than words; ligatures and extension of syllables belong to the domain of regular song, and are excluded from the recitative. (4) Finally, the recitative is not bound to any particular key; it often happens that by means of the recitative a modulation into a distant key is effected between two different movements; besides, in passionate recitatives, changes of harmony may more often appear than would be advisable in a systematic piece.

With regard to the accompaniment of the recitative we recognize (1) the "secco," or simple, and (2) the "accompagnato," the fully accompanied recitative. 1. In the secco the change of harmony is merely marked by the starting of the chords; in olden time the double-bass gave the bass tone, and the spinet or harpsichord supplemented the harmony. The union of the spinet (harpsichord) and double-bass may have been more satisfactory than that of a piano-forte with the double-bass. In other instances one double-bass and several violoncellos gave the chord, the violoncello generally resting for some time on the top note:

This kind of accompaniment, although not under all circumstances sufficient, was more applicable in the church than in the concert-room or opera. In (2) the accompaniment shows itself in two kinds—(a) the stringed instruments sustain the chords, whilst the singer performs the recitative; changes of harmony may take place within the bar in common time on the first and third crotchets, but such modulations are only to be used sparingly, in so far as they are likely to interfere with the distinctness of the recitation; (b) the instruments, after having given the key, perform in the pauses (cæsuras) of the recitative short passages, which assist in giving to the recitative a higher characteristic meaning. (A beautiful example of this kind is the recitative to Donna Anna's aria "Crudele," in Mozart's "Don Giovanni.")

If there occur in the course of a recitative passages of a more lyrical expression the composer generally substitutes for the mere reciting a short cantabile, and then the recitative is called "recitativo arioso" (see Arioso). Although in the recitativo arioso the importance of the declamation recedes for a little while in order to make room for the more melodious element, it is nevertheless very necessary that the composer should give in the arioso the best and most correct accent to the words which determine the sense of the sentence. The recitation in its first germ is decidedly the oldest manner of expression. The song of all pre-Christian (or civilized) nations must have been a kind of recitation, in so far as the means for an independent melodious life and expression were all wanting; the musical expression was still associated with speech and to rhythmical movements of the body, but even in the Christian era it took long until the tone freed itself from the word, and it may safely be asserted that the method applied to singing the Psalms initiated the recitative in the modern sense. At about 1600 the Opera was invented,* and it became a matter of the utmost necessity to have a style of performance better suited to a lively action. Although at first rather stiff and uncouth, this method (as has been shown by our modern recitative) was capable of improvement. (Compare Winterfeld, "Gabrieli," vol. ii. p. 19; Kiesewetter, "Weltliche Gesänge," p. 24.) The recitative was much improved by Monteverde, also by Carissimi and Alessandro Scarlatti. It is said that the last-named composer invented the Recitativo accompagnato. In German Passion-music and in similar sacred dramatic works the recitative for a long time resembled the psalmody. The shortest example will show this difference :—

RECITATIVE FROM THE ORATORIO "JEPHTHA."

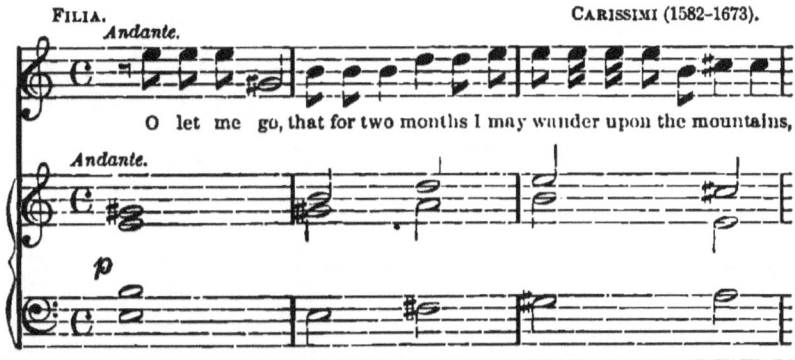

* About 1580 a society of artists and amateurs was formed at Florence in the house of Giovanni Bardi, Count de Vernio. This society aimed at improving the musical art, and desired to effect a revival (Wiederbelebung) of the old Greek recitation in the dramas. This society consisted of the amateurs Vincenzio Galilei, Giacomo Corsi, Pietro Strozzi, the poet Ottavio Rinuccini, and the musical composers Emilio del Cavalieri, Giacomo Peri, and Giulio Caccini. The first fruit of their studies and labors was "the first" lyrical opera, " Daphne," poetry by Rinuccini, performed for the first time in 1594, at Florence. This work was soon followed by the first tragic opera, "Orfeus e Euridice," poetry by Rinuccini, music by Peri and Caccini. After this came " Il Satiro " and "La Disperazione di Filano," both with music by Cavalieri. Almost at the same time Orazio Vecchi tried a kind of *comic* opera, which was performed in 1594, at Modena, under the name "L' Antiparnasso," commedia armonica. The vocal part consisted at that time only of recitatives, and the orchestra of a spinet, tenor-violins, guitars, harps, small organs, fifes, horns, and trumpets — which, however, did not perform according to stated rule.

MUSICAL FORMS.

RECITATIVE FROM THE "HISTORIA DER SIEGREICHEN UND FRÖHLICHEN AUFERSTEHUNG."

HEINRICH SCHÜTZ (1585–1672).

ARIA.

(A.) In a general sense, an aria is every tuneful air or melody which has a certain definite form, and is not merely a recitation. Although the word Aria was first applied to vocal music only, it was later also used for melodious pieces of instrumental music (See Handel's and Sebastian Bach's Suites). In the sixteenth and seventeenth centuries the word Aria was applied to a cheerful song, which was set for one or more voices. The aria for one voice was set only with a simple thorough-bass (*basso continuo*); that set for several voices was, when the supplementary voices were absent, sung in the principal part, and the missing vocal parts played by instruments. In Italy Aria means also a song; and this meaning is still accepted by some parts of the German people. Prætorius (1619) in his "Syntagma," vol. iii. p. 17, says: "*Aria vel Air* is a pretty tune or melody, which any one sings without notes; it is also a secular song with fine and graceful words."

And these pretty songs the Italians call now also "Schertzi." Mattheson ("Neu eröffnetes Orchestra," p. 179, 1713) says: "An aria is generally any melody performed either *vocaliter* or *instrumentaliter*, but *in specie;* it is a melody that is sung and which has to direct itself after the character of the words. (See also Aria in Instrumental music.)

(B.) The aria in the special sense, as lyrical dramatic tone-form, appears in two kinds — namely, as grand aria with the da capo (repetition), or with a free repetition. The first is the older form, the second the more modern one, actually a consequence of the first.

The structure of the (1) *Grand Aria* is the following: the words consist of two sentences, of which the first expresses the general feeling; the second, however, a particular feature of this feeling; in other arias the words are merely arranged in two distinct sentences, of which the first is repeated, for example in Handel's "Judas Maccabœus":

1.
From mighty kings he took the spoil;
And with his acts made Judah smile.

2.
Judah rejoiceth in his name,
And triumphs in her hero's fame.

According to this dualism (Zweitheiligkeit) of the poem, the melody appears also in two parts.

The (*a*) first part begins with the instrumental prelude (Symphony, Ritornello), which contains already the melody; this prelude is followed by the voice, which brings the melody first simple and unadorned; this melody is afterwards divided into smaller parts, which alternate with the orchestra; it is also customary to modulate into the dominant or relative minor or major key; by means of modulation the return to the tonic is resumed; and after (not always necessary) a postlude the first part closes in the tonic. (*b*) The second part is generally shorter and has no repetition, and is therefore simply sung in a straightforward manner, interspersed with short interludes of the orchestra, so as to allow the singer time for rest. When the singer has finished the second part the orchestra takes up the prelude or ritornello, and then comes the (*c*) da capo, which is merely the repetition of the first part up to its close in the principal key (tonic). The key of the second part is generally one closely related to that of the first part. It was also customary to compose the first part as an allegro in common time, and to set the second part in slower and triple time. Although this maxim was often followed out, it could not be regarded as an indispensable or unalterable rule.

STRUCTURE OF THE GRAND ARIA.

PART I. (*a*.)	PART II. (*b*.)	PART III. (*c*.)
Instrumental. Prelude or Ritornello. Principal melody. Modulation into the dominant. Return to the tonic with variation. Short instrumental postlude.	Second melody without elaboration. Much shorter and more concise than Part I.	Da Capo. Prelude or Ritornello. Repetition *in toto* of Part I., with new variation of principal melody.

It will be remarked that this form is very similar to, nay almost identical with, a minuet and trio, in a sonata or symphony.

As the first part was conceived in a much broader style and intended to portray the chief sentiment, it was also here that the performer tried to show his vocal skill. It might be said that the first part belonged to the singer, the second again to the composer, in so far as no ornaments were introduced in the second part, and as the harmonization was generally richer and more interesting than that of the first part. It was the duty of the singer to elaborate every repetition of the principal melody, and particularly to show, by means of well-invented variations, the da capo in a new and different light. The pleasure of the public in these variations and ornamentations was so great, that, naturally enough, the chief character of the music and the words was overlooked, and the aria became merely a welcome means of showing off technical skill. From this undue prominence of vocal execution resulted the so-called "Aria di bravura" (Coloraturarie) which possesses no value at all as a dramatic form and exists merely to exhibit the easy and fluent execution of the singer. (Compare Rossini's arias in "Semiramide," "Barbiere," etc.) The invention of the grand aria with the da capo is generally attributed to Alessandro Scarlatti (1650–1725), although, according to Arteaga, Benedetto Ferrari (della Tiorba, 1597–1681), a composer of the seventeenth century who lived before A. Scarlatti, is the real inventor of this form.

The following shows how these variations were constructed:—

ARIA "SE COSTANTE OGNOR T' AMAI."

LAMPARELLI.

2. *The Aria in the free form.* —In as far as the Aria is the exponent of a particular personal feeling, which feeling emanates from the character and individuality of a person, and cannot be expressed after a set pattern, or according to an established scheme, it was felt that the form of the grand aria was, more particularly with regard to dramatic feeling, entirely insufficient. For this reason the later composers conceived the necessity of adhering more strictly to the sense of the words, which, again portrayed the sentiment at much greater length than was the case formerly. For this reason the strict form of the grand aria was abandoned and a free form adopted; consequently the form of the dramatic or free aria shows itself in as many different kinds as the different dramatic situations demand for their effective portrayal. As a splendid example of a dramatic aria may be cited Agatha's aria in Weber's "Freischütz," "Nie nahte mir der Schlummer" ("Softly sighs"). Among all the composers who still adhered to the rigorous form, none has been so successful in infusing dramatic feeling into it as Mozart.

(c.) With regard to the æsthetic value, beauty, and necessity of the aria, it may be observed that it is as necessary and indispensable in the opera or oratorio as the monologue is in the play. The feelings expressed in an aria are actually the result of preceding incidents. These feelings must be put in a concise form in order to be understood; were they merely presented in the form of a recitative the listener would not be so deeply impressed by them. It may therefore be said that the aria (particularly the dramatic aria) is the exposition of the innermost feelings that, as has been mentioned before, are the results of preceding dramatic situations of a person whose feelings are actually of importance and interest to the whole story. The sacred aria may perhaps not claim such direct necessity, in as far as it contemplates at times the situation from a more objective (outward) point of view. The dramatic aria again is the musical portrayal of a subjective (individual) feeling. The correct and artistic union of the melismatic (ornamental) with the syllabic treatment in the aria is a test of great, nay, rare ability. Mozart, again, has here excelled all other composers in this particular feature.

(D.) Some other forms of arias are (1) the already-mentioned aria di bravura (see Coloratura). This kind of aria is treated in a more melismatic (figured, ornamented) style; its aim and intention are to offer the singer a means of showing his skill in turns, shakes, runs, etc.; (2) the church aria (aria di chiesa) is generally found in a sacred cantata or a Passion-music, or exists also as an independent piece (compare Stradella's celebrated air, "Se' i miei sospiri"). Its musical structure is generally that of the grand aria with the da capo; its expression, however, is more lyrical, the outpourings of a "devout soul," or more like the interpretation of the feelings of a whole community presented in an objective manner. Its style is more syllabic than melismatic, in as far as the sacred word appears more important, and ought thus to be better understood. Any exhibition of passion is here excluded, indeed the "aria di chiesa" is more of a meditative and contemplative, than a strongly-expressed individual character.

3. The *Concert Aria* (aria di concerto) came into fashion towards the end of last century. Partly resting on the form of the grand aria, again profiting by the improved structure of the dramatic aria, and at times using the brilliant features of the aria di bravura, it is

actually a kind of independent "scena," something like an instrumental solo. The aria di concerto is generally preceded by a recitative. Of Mozart we possess twelve such scenas; of Beethoven, the well-known scena and aria "Ah, perfido;" of Mendelssohn, the Concert aria, Op. 94.

4. The *Aria buffa* is a comic aria. Splendid examples of this style, in which mostly Italian composers excelled, are Figaro's aria in Rossini's "Barbiere di Siviglia;" also Masetto's aria "Metà di voi qua vadano;" Don Giovanni's aria, "Finch' han dal vino;" Leporello's aria "Mandamina" in Mozart's "Don Giovanni;" Figaro's aria in C major in the same composer's opera, "Le Nozze di Figaro." It will be observed that in all these examples each note has a syllable, and that the style is more *parlante* (speaking) than sustained or florid.

ARIETTA.

This is a small and shorter kind of aria; the arietta has no second part, and its whole structure is planned in smaller dimensions. In operas the arietta describes less important and less deep feelings, which have only a transient value. Zerlina's two ariettas in Mozart's "Don Giovanni" are splendid examples.

ARIOSO.

This holds its place as a kind of melody which stands between recitative and aria. It may happen that some parts of the secco (recitativo) approach more the lyrical domain, unless these feelings last for any longer time, in which case the composer changes the recitativo into an arioso, an expressive melody, to be sung in strict time. The orchestral accompaniment appears in greater prominence, and the melodious life becomes paramount. It was customary to finish a long recitativo with an arioso, in which the preceding sentiments are, so to say, concentrated. Again, if the situation is a lyrical one, the arioso appears as a kind of song; with Handel it is used as a kind of dialogue between two persons, expressing a feeling in which they unite or which they exhibit singly in turn. A kind of mixture of the secco (recitativo) and arioso has been often applied by Bach, who brought this style to the greatest perfection. Very interesting examples are also to be found in Heinrich Schütz's (1585-1672) "Seven Words."

CAVATA, CAVATINA.

(*a*) A kind of aria for a single voice, which differs from the ordinary aria in the following points: the cavatina is shorter, and consists only of one part, is not repeated, but has generally a longer text than the aria; for this reason there are no repetitions of the words, or at any rate very few may occur. According to its contents, the cavatina is more adapted to a meditative or contemplative than to a passionate expression. Prolongations of syllables or melismas (florid vocalization) are either entirely avoided or only used in exceptional cases. The melody of the cavatina is generally simple, occupying a middle place between that of the aria and arioso, and possesses at times a reciting quality. (*b*) Cavatina is also called an arioso at the end of a recitative, in which the feeling is concentrated, and the expression becomes that of a tuneful agreeable melody. (See Matthe⁓⁓. "Critica mus.," vol. ii. p. 146.)

COLORATURA.

This is a name given to divisions, runs, trills, cadenzas, and other florid passages in vocal music; for instance in the aria of Manoah, "Thy glorious deeds inspir'd my tongue" (Handel's "Samson"):—

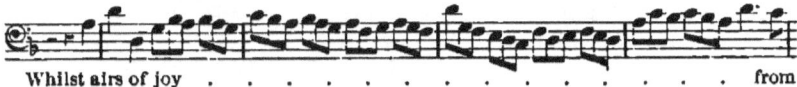

Whilst airs of joy . . . . from

We find already indications of the application of coloratura in the operatic music of Cavalli and Cesti, about 1640. When the coloratura is artistically employed, it is able to serve as an accessory of formal beauty; through it the melody may become less rigid, it receives a richer ornamentation, and may even produce surprising and charming effects. A beautiful example of this kind is Haydn's aria "With verdure clad." But on the other hand, the singers, generally poor musicians, have abused this otherwise legitimate effect, and have in many instances destroyed, by its false application and sometimes anachronistic use, the original effect of the piece, and have even cruelly interfered and destroyed the intended purpose of the composer. In former times, the good opera-singers were expected to compose the coloraturas themselves, the composer merely offering in his aria the skeleton, which had to be adorned and supplemented by the coloratura of the performing singer; at present the singers have lost this art to a great extent, and for this reason the few composers who are still inclined to that obsolete manner of writing, compose the coloraturas themselves. Burney, in his Diary, gives an amusing description of the coloratura used by the celebrated singer Farinelli, in his competition (Rome, 1723) with a trumpeter.

DUET.

(Ital. *duetto*.)

A *Duet* is a piece for two voices, both of which are principal voices in so far as each takes the same important part in the development and characteristic execution of the principal idea. An instrumental duet is generally called *duo*, so as to mark the difference between it and the vocal duet. There is also a difference between a duet and a two-part song; the latter is merely a harmonious strengthening of a melody by using another voice part in intervals that seconds the melody; the duet, however, is always written in a polyphonic style, each part being individually developed as well in point of rhythm as design. We find, therefore, that the duet represents two persons, who, although uniting in the desire of attaining a certain aim, have each their own individual feeling concerning it, and when the union is effected it comes about by a completely free resolve and not by the submission of one party to the other. The duet is divided into the (*a*) chamber duet and (*b*) the dramatic dialogue. The chamber or art-duet (Kunstduet) is the most artistic and most refined of all polyphonic forms which came into use towards the middle of the seventeenth century; it is not merely a component part of a longer composition, but an independent piece. Its form is tolerably varied; it may consist of one or more movements. If it has only one movement ' form of it is like the aria with the da capo (see Aria.) If it consists of several movements, recitatives and solos are introduced, indeed it becomes a regular "scena" (see Scena); the text is generally more lyric than dramatic. To understand the aim, construction, and characteristic form of these duets better, it is advisable to read in Dr. Chrysander's "Life of Handel," vol. ii. p. 328, the remarks about the duets of Steffani (1655-1730), and to compare afterwards Steffani's duets: "Forma un mare di pianto," "Luci bella non tanta," "Placidissime catene." (*b*) The dramatic duet: In this two persons represent different sentiments, or if they represent the same feeling, they express it in a totally different characteristic manner; whilst the chamber duet relies on the aria form; the dramatic duet has no certain form, and depends almost entirely on the dramatic situation. Compare the pithy remarks of J. C. Lobe, "Lehrbuch der musikalischen Komposition," vol. iv. pp. 236-271, and analyze the duet between Don Ottavio and Donna Anna in Mozart's "Don Giovanni" (act 1, No. 2), and Agatha and Annchen's duet "Schelm halt fest," in Weber's "Freischütz" (act 2). (See also Dialogue.)

DIALOGO (DIALOGUE).

Musical dialogue is strictly speaking a duet, which in the form of its composition resembles spoken dialogue. In sacred music it is applied in the form of an aria, sung in turn by each of the two voices, and these voices join, at the end, in a kind of choral. All the arias in oratorios, cantatas, Passions, operas, that are accompanied by an obbligato instrument, such as the violin, oboe di caccia, corno inglese, clarinet, flute, etc., may be included among dialogues, although this term has not yet been generally adopted. (See for example the aria "Erbarme dich mein Gott" in Sebastian Bach's "Passion of St. Matthew;" Mozart's aria "Non più di fiori," in F major, in his "Clemenza di Tito," etc.)

CHORUS.

Chorus (Ger. *Chor;* Fr. *Chœur;* Ital. *Coro*) means a company, a multitude of persons. A musical piece for several voice parts, in which each part is not performed by a single or solo singer but by several persons; each voice part so performed is called a chorus part. (*a*) According to æsthetic ideas a chorus is the united expression of a number of individuals whose feeling is impressed by an event or idea in so thoroughly uniform a manner, that all of them unite in the same expression. For this reason the contents of a chorus must be such that not only the individual but the company approves of it, and the expression becomes actually an objective one. As solo singing is the expression of the single person's feeling, just so is the chorus the expression of the feeling of a community or congregation. The chorus parts differ from each other through the character and compass of their voices—treble, alto, tenor and bass; which different voice parts have not inaptly been compared to the different stages of the life of both sexes. By the number of persons which perform each chorus part, any prominence of personality (individuality) ceases, and each part again is fused into the whole of the chorus. A working out in detail of the different phases of feeling or individualizing them, as it happens in the aria, is in the chorus not only superfluous but inadmissible; on the other hand there may be a different expression given to one particular part with regard to the others. The great effect, the mighty power, of a chorus consists in the strength and grandeur of the collective expression, in the massiveness of tone brought about by the number of performers all uniting in one task. Such is the might that we admire in the choruses of Schütz (see his "Passion" from the Four Evangelists), Sebastian Bach, and Handel. (*b*) The essential and real style of the chorus is imitatory and fugal; the chief form of the chorus is actually the fugue, in which all parts participate with equal right in the execution of the set task. Other styles are the *rigorous* and the *free*. The rigorous style adopts the fugal treatment, and relies on the system of double counterpoint; the free style is more like the arioso, or, again, the dramatic expression. Rigorous choruses need not only appear in oratorios or sacred compositions; they may be also applied in the opera or secular cantata, madrigals, and glees. The work which contains almost all possible forms of choruses is undoubtedly Sebastian Bach's "Passion of St. Matthew," from the most artistically figured chorus with canto fermo down to the turbæ, the expression of the enraged people. Next to this admirable work Handel's "Israel in Egypt" affords the most interesting material for deep and earnest study. (*c*) Formal construction: the commonly-applied form for the lyrical chorus is that of the aria in two parts with the da capo (see Aria). For this reason these choruses were sometimes called Aria-choruses.

In dramatic works (such as oratorios) the form of the chorus is dependent of the situation; some are quite short, like the turbæ (see Schütz, Sebastian Bach, Mendelssohn's "St. Paul," etc.). In strictly sacred music the so-called choral chorus, or a chorus with the choral as canto fermo, is that which is mostly found. (*d*) The chorus à cappella, without any accompaniment (or if with accompaniment, the instruments—generally stringed instruments—playing the different parts of the chorus; namely, violino 1mo (soprano), violino 2do (alto), viola (tenor), violoncello, and double-bass (basso). In the chorus à cappella the melody has a more prominent part. In some choruses the voice parts are simple, without any ornamentation or figures, which latter are furnished by the orchestra; a beautiful example of this kind is Mendelssohn's expressive chorus in "St. Paul," "Happy and blest are they." Again, in some choruses (see Bach's Mass in B minor and some of Handel's oratorios) the execution is very florid and founded on a regular coloratura.

(*e*) With regard to the number of parts employed, the chorus is very different. We have choruses from three to twelve, sixteen, and (in old Italian compositions) more parts; the normal number, and at the same time most common, is the four-part chorus. In choruses of five, six, seven, or eight parts the division of the respective parts depends upon the effect the composer wishes to obtain; divided altos and basses produce a greater effect of dignity and earnestness, divided sopranos and tenors again give the expression of brightness and splendor. In eight-part chorus the parts are either all together as one whole, or are divided in two choruses of four parts each, thus forming a double chorus.

Soprano and alto are mostly sung by female voices, but at times they are also mixed or entirely sung by boys; female voices produce a softer, more melodious, but at the same time more sensual effect;

the voices of boys have a more astringent, inflexible, but more piercing and energetic tone-color and are entirely passionless. The mixture of female with boys' voices is of the happiest effect. Less so is the mixture of male contraltos with female; although the manner of employing the contralto in so low a register as was used by the old Italian writers of the time of Palestrina up to Bach and Handel, necessitated this method. In some countries the employment of female voices in the church was thought inadmissible, and some writers mention as a reason for this rigorous rule the words of St. Paul, in his Epistle to the Corinthians, xiv. 43, "Let your women keep silence in the churches, for it is not permitted unto them to speak." It was, so it is reported, Cyrillus, Bishop of Jerusalem (A.D. 386), who, on the strength of St. Paul's direction forbade the participation of women in the musical church service, but this restriction cannot have been universal, in so far as in convents women had necessarily to sing the service (compare Forkel's History, vol ii. p. 140).

(*f*) The words for the chorus are generally a short, but terse sentence, which explains the sense in the most concise and most intelligible manner, without any undue elaboration or ornamentation. If the chorus has a second part or a fugue, the work must consist of two sentences, used alternately, so as to avoid monotony.

(*g*) A chorus consisting of female and male voices is called a *mixed* chorus. This kind is of all the most desirable, as it offers not only the greatest variety with regard to the characteristic tone-colors, but allows of a much freer treatment, in as far as the respective voice parts are not so close as they would be in a chorus written only for female or male voices.*

According to Isidorus, the word *Chorus* has its derivation from *corona*, in as far as the singers of olden times were placed round the altar in the form of a crown or wreath (*corona constantium*).

CANTATA.

(Ital. *cantare*, to sing.)

A *Cantata* is a form which belongs to vocal music, and by which we generally understand a composition of several pieces, which comprise choruses, recitatives, and arias. This meaning is derived particularly from the form of Sebastian Bach's great church cantatas; this form, however, was preceded by two different kinds of cantata form, and therefore it is not easy to define clearly the meaning of the word Cantata. With regard to its development as a form it must be mentioned that some composers treated it as a lyrical piece for one voice (for example, Mozart's cantata for one voice, "Die ihr des unermesslichen Weltall's Schöpfer ehrt"); some other composers again looked at it from the most dramatic point of view; with others again the cantata appears almost identical with the oratorio; sometimes again it shows itself as a piece not unlike a song or an ode; at times it appears again as a lyrical composition with a dramatic expression, with or without a mixture of the epic element, written for a solo voice or

---

* Compare the following works:—Nägeli (Hans Georg), "Chor Gesangschule:" Leipzig: Fr. Fleischer, 1821. Häser (August Ferdinand), "Chor Gesangschule;" German and French; Mayence: Schott. Choron (Alexandre Etienne), "Méthode concertante de Plein-chant," etc.; Paris, 1819.

for a chorus. All cantatas, however, unite in this—that they absolutely require an instrumental accompaniment, and that the poetry is in the lyrical style. The chief difference between the opera, oratorio, and the cantata is, that in the first two a regular dramatic action is played before or related to us; whilst the cantata expresses only sentiments, brought about by the meditation upon great events, heroic deeds, scenes of nature, contemplations of divine might, moral subjects, etc. The words of the cantata are founded on events of all possible time and kind, on supernatural and natural incidents, on the Christian faith, or the worship of the ancient mythology, etc. The aim of the cantata is actually the glorification or apotheosis of illustrious persons, or stirring events; the lyrical expression of the cantata, however, shows itself not so purely personal as in the song, but in a more objective, general manner. Oratorio and cantata may be often confounded; there are oratorios which are more like cantatas, and *vice versâ*. It is a great mistake to take the respective length of either oratorio or cantata as decisive for the name; there is, for example, Haydn's cantata "The Seasons," of the length and dimensions of an oratorio; again, there are oratorios so short, that they might be considered to be cantatas. The oratorio has a style of its own; it stands between secular and sacred music; it is secular in so far as it does not exclude dramatic life and human passion; again it is sacred, because its subjects and stories are taken from the Bible, although its musical expression is not so rigorous and solemnly tranquil as that of the regular sacred music, which forbids the delineation of human passion. The cantata does not, like the oratorio, present persons or characters; a personification will merely approach the "devout soul," but this again represents in the church cantata merely the sentiments of the community. (See Winterfeld, "Kunst des evangelische Kirchengesanges.")

According to its chief characteristics or principal expression we class the cantata as an *ode-like cantata* (for one single voice), or as a *chamber cantata*, requiring several performers, and lastly as a *great cantata*, which has all the apparatus of the oratorio—grand orchestra, chorus, and solo voices. The formerly much used *Trauer cantate*, funeral cantata (a kind of short requiem) belongs to the form of the great cantata, and differs only in the characteristic expression; whilst the great cantata has a grand, majestic, broad, and lofty expression; the funeral cantata relies on a more pathetic, mournful, and quiet expression. In the cantata the influence of the madrigal and motet is more observable than in the oratorio. As the choruses of a cantata lack dramatic life, the composer excels more in an artistically refined treatment of counterpoint. The origin of the simple cantata is to be sought in Italy, about 1600; the inventor of the chamber cantata was Carissimi, who flourished in Rome between 1635 and 1672. The form of the great cantata was principally applied by John Sebastian Bach, who left us splendid examples of this style. It may be remarked that Handel's anthems are in fact sacred cantatas.

CANTATINA, OR CANTATILLE.

This means a smaller form of cantata, with which it corresponded in its various features, excepting that the whole structure was on a smaller scale and the various parts less elaborated. Like the cantata it is accompanied by instruments.

QUODLIBET.

(Ital., *Mischianza;* Ger., *Mansch.*)

Prætorius, in his "Syntagma," vol. iii. p. 18, describes a quodlibet as "a mixture of all possible herbs; of many various motets, madrigals, and other secular and humorous songs; separate parts are taken, with half a line or a whole line of a text, and from these rags and fragments a new (Peltz) is patched together." Some writers intentionally corrupted not only the melodies but also the words, and thus obtained a comical and burlesque effect. National and sacred songs were mostly applied to this kind of amusement. To give an idea of a regular quodlibet, we select one that was sung by the members of the Bach family at their annual meetings. (See Hilgenfeldt's "Biography of Sebastian Bach," p. 8; Leipzig, 1850. See also Quodlibet in Instrumental music.)

DAS VATER UNSER. (The Lord's Prayer.)

DER GLAUBE. (The Creed.)

LOBGESANG AUF DAS OSTERFEST. (Song of Praise for Easter.)

LIED VON DER TAUFE. (Christening Song.)

DIE ZEHEN GEBOT KÜRZERGEFASST. (The Ten Commandments summarized.)

II.

SECULAR FORMS.

SONG.

The name *Song* generally suggests a secular form. In its various meanings it signifies a musical utterance by a human being, a bird, etc.; also, a trifle or thing of little moment, as in the phrase "bought for a song." Owing to its versatility, however, it can also adapt itself to the expression of religious feelings. To give an accurate definition of the word Song in its special meaning (*Lied* in German, *chanson* in French, *canzone* or *canzonetta* in Italian) is not an easy task. We have here to consider what a song should be and what qualities it ought to possess—and to enumerate the different kinds of songs. The Song belongs chiefly to the lyrical domain of musical art,[*] and is generally devoted to the illustration of some separate thought—the stillness of night, the beauty of spring, the worth of liberty, etc. The more clearly a song can be made to express an inward feeling, the greater will naturally be its value, popularity, and effect. The expression of a song is mostly that of pure joy, of hope, of consolation. Thus in the Scriptures the idea of the hills breaking out into singing, the waste places of Jerusalem singing together, the singing a new song unto the Lord continually occurs as an expression of joy, happiness, consolation, and triumph. It can also be made to describe anything with which our fancy is greatly occupied. For these reasons the form of the song is generally much more *cantabile* than other vocal forms. The chief requirements of the song are completeness in the form of the poem, an easy flowing metre, and an agreeably striking rhythm. We see these conditions thoroughly fulfilled in Shakespeare's songs, such as "Hark, hark, the lark," etc.

On the other hand, the song does not often possess brilliancy, splendor, and grandeur; and for this reason it is calculated rather to excite our sympathies than to arouse wonder. A good song must moreover exhibit simplicity, quietness, and truth of expression, a moderate compass, and an absolute musical representation of the idea of the words. These conditions are exceedingly difficult to fulfil. At first sight it would seem an easy task to compose a good song; but it may be taken for granted that those songs which sound most simple, and strike our heart at once, were produced with the greatest labor

---

[*] Franz Schubert's celebrated songs: "Margaret at the Spinning-wheel," Nachtstück (Op. 36, No. 2), "Willkomm und Abschied" (Op. 56, No. 1), "The young Nun," "Memnon," "Death and the Girl," "By the Sea," "Andie Leyer;" and Robert Schumann's not less celebrated songs: "Lurline" (Waldesgespräch), "Beauteous Cradle" (Schöne Wiege), "A Poet's Love" (Ich grolle nicht)—may be said to make an exception to this rule; in these the *dramatic* feeling supersedes the *lyrical* expression, and it might be asserted that these songs form a connecting link between the lyrical and dramatic art. On the other hand, Schubert, in many of his songs, presents such rich, characteristic and descriptive accompaniments, that the term *Art-song* would here not be misapplied.

and thougnt. As examples may be taken Mozart's "Violet," Schubert's "Wanderer," Mendelssohn's "On Song's bright pinions," and Schumann's "Devotion"—songs which, with all their simplicity, show evidence of an extraordinarily acute and correct musical feeling in the composers. To keep a song within the right limits, to balance every part of it in absolute proportion, is no easy task; and therefore a good song is, in spite of its shortness, a great work of art. All possible scientific accomplishments and contrapuntal studies will not suffice to give the true, the absolutely correct tone of expression. A really good song must find an echo in the heart; it must vibrate in our innermost feelings; it must move us involuntarily to repeat it ourselves. If we examine the different kinds of songs we possess (we can count them by tens of thousands) we shall find that the oldest songs celebrated religion, war, and also hunting and athletic sports. The religious songs, particularly, existed in olden times in great numbers. St. Paul says, "Let the word of Christ dwell in you richly in all wisdom, teaching and admonishing one another in psalms and hymns and spiritual songs, singing with grace in your hearts to the Lord."

Love-songs date from the time of the minstrels, troubadours, and minnesingers. England, France, Spain, and Germany possess a rich treasure of these mediæval songs; and these songs contributed greatly to soften and improve the harsh and barbarous manners of the feudal times.

But, though song-writing is a secular form, it contains a sacred department. The *Sacred Song* demands, besides a gentle and devout musical expression, wise and lofty words.

CHANSON.

(From *chanter*, to sing; Ital. *canzona*.)

The *Chanson* is a short lyrical vocal piece, indeed, a song. The expression of the modern French chanson is, however, not the same as that of the German song (Lied). Firstly, the chanson has only a melody of the length of one verse, which is not always to be found in the German song; secondly, the chanson does not always express a subjective or individual feeling, but chooses generally a theme that is able to reveal itself in an epigrammatic and pointed manner; it shows its context in each verse as a new and differently expressed subject, and tries to connect at the end of each verse its different expression in a *refrain*, or *ritornelle*, which closes each verse in a happy, unexpected and spirited manner. German songs constructed in a similar manner are called "Strophen-Lieder." There are chansons for almost all events of family or public life, such as *chansons d'amour* (love songs); *chansons à boire ou rondes de tables* (drinking songs); *chansons pastorales ou rustiques* (pastoral or rustic songs); *chansons balladées* (ballads); *chansons pour danser* (dance songs, such as musettes, gavottes, branles, minuets); *chansons guerrières* (war or military songs) —a beautiful example of this kind is the "Chanson de Roland;" *chansons patriotiques* (patriotic songs); *chansons réligieuses* (sacred songs); *chansons satiriques* (satirical songs). Under this last head come the celebrated Mazarinades, satires directed against Cardinal Mazarin, in the time of the Fronde riots. The number of the Mazarinades was very great. C. Moreau (1850), in his "Bibliographie des Mazarinades," enumerates about four thousand. Another kind of French song was called "*les Brunettes*." Diderot and d'Alembert, in their Encyclopædia, give the following description of the word "brunette." "It is a sort of song in which the air is easy and simple, and the style gallant and natural, sometimes tender, and often playful. It is so called because it often happens that in such a song the poet, addressing himself to a young girl, has given her the name of 'brunette'—dark-haired little one."

(Compare for further instruction: J. B. Wekerlin, "Echos du Temps passé," 3 vols.; Paris: Flaxland. Schneider (K. E.), "Das musikalische Lied in geschichtlicher Entwickelung;" Leipzig: Breitkopf and Härtel, 1863.)

The French also excel greatly in their *Noëls* (Christmas carols). They possess a great number of them, all written in a simple, unpretending style. The works which contain the best specimens are:—

"La Philomèle séraphique." En la 1ère partie elle chante les dévots et ardans soupirs de l'âme pénitente qui s'achemine à la vraye perfection; en la 2me, la "Christiade," spécialement les mystères de la Passion; en la 3me la "Mariade," avec les mystères du Rosaire; en la 4me les cantiques de plusieurs saintes, tous en forme d'oraison et de méditation, sur les airs les plus nouveaux choisis des principaux auteurs de ce temps, par Frère Jean l'Évangéliste d'Arras, prédicateur capucin. Tournay, 1640.

"Noëls dijonnais" (1700), republished at Dijon, 1858.
"Noëls bourguignons" (1701.) These noëls were not sung in church, but at home, round the fireside.
"Noëls maconnais" (1720).

MAGGIOLATA.

A song in praise of the recurring spring, which the young men used to sing in the first days of May, round a tree planted for the purpose, before the houses of their beloved ones. This habit was particularly popular in Florence. The phrase "*cantare il maggio*" originated in this custom. (See Nemeitz, "Nachlese besonderer Nachrichten aus Italien.")

BALLAD, BALLADE, BALLATA.

The word *Ballad* is derived from the Italian *ballo*, a dance. Already in the twelfth century the old ballata, a short lyrical song, was frequently sung as an accompaniment to the dance. In the popular songs of England and Scotland the word Ballad originally designated a song connected with some heroic myth, and afterwards it came to mean a song descriptive of some event. The early English literature is peculiarly rich in ballads from the time of the Saxons downward. ("Chevy Chase," the ballads of "Robin Hood," the Scottish "Sir Patrick Spens;" in 1560 nearly eight hundred ballads were entered at Stationers' Hall; the number from the reign of Henry VIII, to the year 1700, printed without music, is stated at ten thousand). The popular ballad or song of the people has only one melody, which is repeated with every strophe and the accompaniment remains the same. The composer accordingly had to produce a melody, which should express the general idea of the poem, as he could not vary the matter to express the separate features of particular verses. Each ballad had not its own tune; it was customary to write new ballads upon wonderful or startling events as they arose, and to sing them to popular melodies. When Shakespeare's inimitable Autolycus comes with his stock of peddler's wares to the sheep-shearing feast, his cniet recommendation is that he brings a goodly store of ballads for the edification of the rustics. "What hast there?" asks the clown. "Ballads?". "Pray now, buy some," entreats the fair Mopsa. "I love a ballad in print, a'-life! for then we are sure they are true." And a very good market Autolycus makes of his musical wares.

Very frequently the ballad was furnished with a burden, consisting of a line, or sometimes several lines, sung in chorus at the end of each verse.

Ariel, in the "Tempest," calls upon the spirits "to bear the burden of his ballad:"—

> Foot it featly here and there,
> And, sweet sprites, the burden bear.

In the burden (or refrain) the original thought or idea of the ballad was frequently emphasized.

The modern ballad has, to a great extent, departed from the simplicity of the original form, the verses being varied in melody and expression, according to the different emotions to be portrayed, as for instance in Goethe's "Erl-king," Bürger's "Leonore," etc. The dramatic element comes prominently forward in the ballad, in which the characters are often represented as speaking in dialogue, in contradistinction to the narrative form, as for instance in the charming old ballad "The Bailiff's Daughter of Islington."

NATIONAL SONGS.

Under *National Songs* may be classed all songs that appeal, in any form, to patriotic feeling. The best example of what a national song ought to be has been furnished by Joseph Haydn in his "God preserve the Emperor." Other good specimens are the "Marseillaise" and the "Russian Hymn." Excellent examples are also found in Weber's songs "Lyre and Sword" and Arne's stirring "Rule Britannia." The popular songs, or songs of the people, are indeed excellent in every country, and are the truest expression of national life and sentiment; for the songs of a nation are a natural result of the manner of life, and also depend greatly on geographical and climatic relations. Thus a nation inhabiting a mountainous country has songs of a livelier and richer character and of more varied expression than the inhabitants of a flat region generally possess. Again, the songs of the Northern nations, as Russians, Swedes, Norwegians, Danes, and Eskimos, are mostly of a melancholy expression; while the Southern nations, such as Spaniards and Italians, and to some extent also the Hungarian, Bohemian, and Slavonic races, combine their songs with dancing. Among the lovely Italian popular songs those of Tuscany claim the highest place. The English, Scotch, and Irish songs are justly celebrated, and have been adapted and utilized by the greatest composers.

Convivial and *Humorous Songs* are a natural consequence of the *Liedertafeln*, or musical convivial associations. The *Liedertafeln* are represented in Great Britain by the madrigal and glee club.

COUPLET.

Couplet, in the general sense, is the repetition of any amount of verses that are sung to the same melody of the first verse. The songs in comic operas or vaudevilles, or burlesques, which the comic actor sings, and in which he alludes in a humorous and sometimes satirical manner to political or social questions of the day are also called Couplets. The same name is given to variations generally added to a chaconne or passacaille. (Compare for instance Couperin's beautiful chaconne "La Ténébreuse.") The episodes that offer relief to the repetitions of the principal subject in a rondo are sometimes termed Couplets.

MADRIGAL.

A composition in three or more parts for voices, without accompaniment; each part being supported by several singers. It is probable that the word Madrigal was originally the name of a short rustic poem, and that it was afterwards given to the music to which such poems were set. A similar process may have taken place with such words as Rondo, Sonnet, Roundelay, Fa la. There are great varieties of style and form amongst madrigals; some consist of a short, simple melody broadly harmonized; others are closely allied in form to the sacred *motet;* some not only include all the devices of counterpoint, but are also divided into distinct movements. The madrigal period may be roughly set down as from 1550 to 1650. Italy and England produced important schools of madrigal writers. Among the English writers, the best are, Dowland, Morley, Ward, Wilbye, Tallis, Weelkes, Benet, Gibbons.

GLEE.

The *Glee* is a form of composition peculiar to the English school of music. The glee is nearly always sung by one voice to a part, and in its purest style is unaccompanied. The separate vocal parts of a glee are as a rule more melodious and less contrapuntal than those of the madrigal, hence it is more capable of tenderness and expression than a madrigal; but less capable of producing broad effects. The glee is essentially a branch of Chamber-music. The best period of the glee was from 1750 to 1830. Since the latter period the introduction of the part-song has to a considerable extent superseded it. Amongst the most successful composers of glees were S. Webbe, Dr. Cooke, Dr. Callcott, R. J. S. Stevens, Reginald Spofforth, Stafford Smith, W. Horsley. A glee of a gentle and quiet character, with words having reference to the charms of rustic life, of friendship, or love, is sometimes called a "serious glee;" while if its words are of a jovial or droll nature it is termed a "cheerful glee." The most fully developed glees consist of several contrasted movements, and in many cases, instead of a vigorous climax, they are brought to a soft and pathetic close.

ROUNDS AND CATCHES.

A *Round* is, strictly speaking, a canon at the unison so constructed that when the parts are written one over the other, as is usually the case, they form one well-defined musical period. To insure a proper cadence, a round sometimes must be finished at some point before the close of the line, in which case a pause is placed to point out the final notes, and is only to be observed when the round is sung for the last time, *e. g.* :—

The Catch was originally merely a round written out in one long line instead of being arranged in score; each voice that entered had therefore to *catch* the point of entry. Afterwards, a catch was a term applied to any round in which the words were capable of a double meaning, according to their accent, or their division between the lines. Catches were much in vogue in the reign of Charles II.

OBSOLETE FORMS OF SONGS.

I.—LAI, LAY, LEICH (*Ger.*)

A song in the popular form in contradistinction to the artistic song or chanson. The name was given originally to the epic and narrative poems of the Anglo-Norman Trouvères, which were sung to Breton popular melodies ("Lais historiques," "Lais de Chevalerie"). Afterwards the name was extended to the popular song generally, whether lyric or narrative; as for instance in the old epic lays which were spread among the people by the menestrels or jongleurs.

II.—CANZONE.

A very old form of song-poem or musical vocal composition, frequently sung by the Troubadours and Minstrels; various in its versification, but generally allied to the Pindaric or Horatian metre, and ordinarily *secular* in its contents; love songs, etc., and composed in the style of a cantata. Sometimes, however, the Canzone was on a sacred subject, and such compositions were called Canzoni spirituali.

III.—CANSON REDONDA.

A roundelay was the name given to a kind of song-poem, sung by the Troubadours, in which the last line of each stanza was repeated as the first line of the next, so that the whole of the stanzas were connected with each other.

PASTORAL.

(1) *Pastoral* is a piece of a simple, rustic expression—a shepherd's song, generally in six-eight time. To this form belong the *Musette* and *Siciliano;* the Siciliano, however, is distinguished from the Pastoral by dotted notes, which are wanting in the pastoral. (2) Pastoral is a short, musical dramatic work, whose subject is taken from the life of shepherds or country people; the music ought to express throughout simplicity and innocence, and must avoid any show of dramatic passion. (3) The name pastoral is also given to pieces of larger dimensions, which owe their existence to impressions received by the composer through country life and scenes, and describe incidents of nature. The noblest example of these kind of pieces is Beethoven's Pastoral Symphony.

LIEDERSPIEL.

This is a play which is interspersed with songs or ballads, a kind of vaudeville; it must not be confounded with a singspiel or operetta, as in the latter recitative and aria and regular scenes are necessary. The liederspiel was invented by John Friedr. Reichardt (1752–1814)—not to be confounded with Gustav Reichardt, the composer of the well-known German national song "Was ist des deutschen Vaterland." J. F. Reichardt was anxious to initiate a simpler, more natural style. His liederspiel "Liebe und Treue" (1800) and "Kunst und Liebe" were very successful.

In England we find this form already represented at a somewhat earlier period by Guy's "Beggar's Opera," and subsequently it appears in such works as "The Quaker," "The Waterman," and "Love in a Village."

MASQUE.

A *Mask* is the name of a secular poem, generally of mythological character, which was either performed on the stage with the aid of a ballet, or merely sung in the concert-room. (See the preface to Handel's "Acis and Galatea" in the third volume of the German Handel Society.)

BURLETTA.

The word comes from the Italian, and designates a comic operetta or farcial play, in which songs are introduced.

OPERA.

The word *Opera* is the plural of the Latin *opus*, and means "works." In a musical sense it may be defined as a work of art, in which music, words, and a visible action, sometimes accompanied by dancing, combine to represent a certain story; the whole being enhanced by the effect of scenery. This story can be either *serious, lyric, romantic,* or *comic.* In the first case the opera is called a grand or tragic opera (*e. g.* "Les Huguenots"), in the second a lyric opera (*e. g.* "La Sonnambula"), in the third a romantic opera (*e. g.* "Der Freischütz"), and in the last a comic opera, or *opera buffa* (*e. g.* "Il Barbiere di Siviglia"). The opera is divided into acts, and these again into scenes, in the regular dramatic style. The music is vocal and instrumental; the vocal part predominates; and the independent instrumental part is confined to the overture, entr'acte, and introductions. The combination of different arts renders the opera a work of great importance, concerning whose position and value in an artistic point of view there has been, and is likely to be, much controversy. The idea of uniting and amalgamating the art of speech, of song, and of action in one work is by no means modern: to produce a work in which all these arts have an equal part, was an object which the ancient Greeks desired to realize. The actual solution of this problem seems to be still very distant; for as each of the separate arts has attained great perfection the idea of subordinating one to another becomes less and less practicable. Each of the fine arts has its particular domain, from which it excludes the sister arts when it has reached a certain stage of freedom and independence. A perfect drama, for instance, will never unite itself to an equally perfect and independently constructed musical work; for they are founded on heterogeneous, and indeed on almost opposite principles. Music, if it is to develop itself according to its specific nature, necessarily claims a perfectly organized and systematic construction; otherwise it sinks to the position of a dependent art, and becomes the handmaid of Poetry. Music expresses our innermost feelings by sounds; but this dogma the drama does not and cannot recognize—for music interrupts the progress of the action in so far as we appreciate the feeling of the hero or of any chief person in the drama through *action* and not *reflection*. In the drama we want to see action, but not to listen to philosophical meditations, which, however, if appropriately and sparingly introduced, can contribute to the general effect. The dramatic action either debars the music from its necessary development into the proper artistic form, or music disturbs the regular life of the drama. In the opera, music can only admit of such a text as will be a vehicle for the expression of emotions and sentiments, to be suitably portrayed by sounds. This does not imply that the story and text ought not to be constructed according to the principal rules of the drama; dramatic plan or design and a perfect *drama* are two quite different things. An opera will always remain a musico-dramatic work of art, and will ever be most effective in expressing the more lyrical sentiments, although it can in a great degree heighten and intensify the dramatic situations; it cannot, however, lend itself to that delineation and development of character in detail which is one of the chief sources of strength in a regular and perfect drama. A reason against the complete representation of a character in the opera may also be that the singers, devoting their chief attention to the voice, are mostly deficient in dramatic education when compared with other actors. The chief aim of the opera must always be a musical one. Thanks to the inexhaustible resources of musical art, the great dramatic composers were capable of imbuing the most varied characters with suitable musical expression; Gluck's, Mozart's, and Weber's operas furnish excellent examples. Some of the finest productions, constructed according to the above-mentioned rule, *that in the opera music should be the principal element*, testify that this dogma is correct. Whether the new tendency to amalgamate all the arts in one *art-work* will act as beneficially as, or even more beneficially than, the older principle, is a question not yet answered to the general satisfaction; it would perhaps be difficult to convince the world that the new productions of Richard Wagner, for instance, are as perfect models of an opera as those of Mozart or Weber—although it cannot be denied that the new product, or "music of the future" as it is generally but erroneously called, possesses a great many elements of truth, correctness, and wonderful effect. It is certainly a highly interesting subject, and one worthy of full, fair, and reasonable discussion, and of earnest examination.

The pieces of which the opera consists are:—

1. Overture.
2. Recitative.
3. Aria.
4. The musical Dramatic Scene.
5. Duet.
6. Terzett (Trio).
7. Ensemble pieces.
8. Chorus.
9. Finale.

About (1) overture, (2) recitative, (3) aria, (5) duet, (8) chorus, see the respective forms.

THE DRAMATIC SCENE.

If the opera contains a situation which is so grand, important, and decisive on the development of the plot, that the form of an aria would actually interfere with the correct comprehension of the situation (in point of psychological truth), and the systematic and well ordered structure of the aria would at the same time be antagonistic to the feelings of curiosity, interest, awe, awakened in the listener—the composer employs instead the dramatic scene, a mixture of recitative and arioso. But not only in the recitative, but also in the arioso the greatest freedom ought to be permitted; the orchestral accompaniment ought to supplement and strengthen the dramatic feeling. A splendid example of this form is the scene No. 14 in Marschner's opera "The Vampyre." (See the masterly analysis of this remarkable scene in Lobe's "Lehrbuch der musikalischen Komposition," vol. iv. pp. 227-236).

TRIO (TERZETT).

In the Trio three persons join in a certain situation, and for this reason it is necessary that, at least in one place in the piece, these three persons sing together, and more particularly so at the end; by this method the composition reaches its necessary climax. This necessity of finishing all three together has been acknowledged by all composers, and in the seventeen trios which the six great operas of Mozart contain, we find only three instances in which we miss the joining of the three voices—namely, the trio between Pamina, Monostatos and Papageno in "Il Flauto magico," the trio between Donna Elvira, Don Giovanni, and Leporello in "Don Giovanni," and the trio (No. 14) between Publius, Vitellia, and Sextus in "La Clemenza di Tito." A careful examination of these three trios will show that there was a sound dramatic reason for this variation of the rule, and that the observation of this reason shows the correct dramatic feeling of the composer.

It is customary to compose the trio in two movements—a slower and a faster movement; but of course the dramatic situation is here, as in all other operatic music, the decisive rule. Beautiful examples of trios are to be found in Rossini's "Guillaume Tell," Weber's "Der Freischütz," Beethoven's "Fidelio," Spohr's "Zemire and Azor," etc.

ENSEMBLE (CONCERTED) PIECES.

The meaning of Ensemble (concerted) Pieces is not certain, or decisive. Indeed, duets and trios are called Ensemble pieces; however, these forms are described by the number of voices employed. Generally ensemble pieces are called the union of four, five, six, and more voices, with or without the supplement of the chorus. The dramatic scene may be constructed in such a manner that two or three persons begin, and are later joined by persons not present in the beginning; but the coming, remaining and leaving of these persons ought to be always the result of a natural necessity, and according to it the composer will mould his musical form. The number and character of pieces constituting the ensemble piece must also depend upon the dramatic situation. If we look for instance at the introduction of "Don Giovanni" we find the ensemble piece consisting of:—

1. *Solo*, Leporello.
2. *Trio*, Donna Anna, Don Giovanni, and Leporello.
3. *Trio*, Don Giovanni, Commendatore, and Leporello.

These three situations are set only in two movements—namely, allegro molto and andante. The sestetto in the same opera consists of:—

1. *Solo*, Donna Elvira.
2. Leporello.
3. Donna Anna and Don Ottavio.
4. Donna Elvira and Leporello.
5. Donna Anna, Donna Elvira, Zerlina, Don Ottavio, Masetto, and Leporello.

These five situations are set in one movement—andante, common time; which, however, becomes a little more animated when the six persons sing together. The Introduction to "Il Flauto magico" is again constructed in the following manner:—

1. Tamino, in a kind of aria, C minor, common time.
2. Three ladies (trio), (*a*) E flat and A flat.
   (*b*) Allegretto, G major, six-eight time.
   (*c*) Allegro, C major, common time.

Other fine examples of ensemble pieces are to be found in Mozart's "Nozze di Figaro," Rossini's "Guillaume Tell" (with chorus), Meyerbeer's "Les Huguenots," Weber's "Der Freischütz" (first and third act), Weber's "Euryanthe" (first act), Wagner's "Lohengrin" (prayer in first act), Donizetti's "Lucia di Lammermoor," etc.

FINALE.

A well planned and successfully carried out finale of the act of an opera is one of the most difficult tasks. The finale comprises actually all possible forms of which the opera consists—from the recitative to the most polyphonic concerted piece. The charm of the Finale is to be found in the fact that situations and places, which appear in the opera divided by the recitative and dialogue, here succeed each other in the greatest variety; and thus lively contrasts, as well in pieces and instrumentation, keep up a warm interest in the listener. The composer has to make at first a precise disposition of all the distinct parts; he has to seek and find all the varieties of the situation; has to make himself thoroughly acquainted with the *character* of each scene, and to find the proper form, key, time, movement, and instrumentation for a true and suitable musical expression. Furthermore, he has to consider which parts of the Finale have to be brought forward with great brilliancy, importance, and force; he has, therefore, to put, so to say, certain parts somewhat in the shade, and has to grasp with a firmness every moment of the dramatic situation that may assist in giving clearness and solid strength to the whole structure. Indeed the composer has not only to command the entire musical apparatus with consummate skill, but has also to be a keen psychological observer. Of all composers Mozart was the one who combined all the necessary requirements for composing a perfect Finale. We subjoin here the scheme of Mozart's Finale to the first act in "Il Flauto magico," and invite the student to make himself acquainted with its music:—

SCENE 1.

1. *Quartette.* Three Genii and Tamino. Larghetto, C major, common time, 38 bars.

SCENE 2.

2. *Recitativo obbligato with short Ariosi.* Tamino, and a voice (the Priests).
3. *Ariette.* Tamino. Andante, C major, common time, 68 bars.
4. *Duet.* Pamina and Papageno. Andante (should be allegro), G major.
5. *Ensemble.* Monostatos and chorus of men, Pamina and Papageno. Allegro, G major, common time, 97 bars.
6. *Duet.* Pamina and Papageno. Andante, G major, common time, 24 bars.
7. *Ensemble and Chorus.* Allegro maestoso, C major, common time, 44 bars.
8. *Duet.* Pamina and Sarastro. Larghetto, F major, common time, 46 bars.
9. *Ensemble and Chorus.* Allegro, F major.
10. *Recitative.* Sarastro.
11. *Final Chorus.* C major, common time, 69 bars.

It will be observed that all the pieces are in common time; but the striking contrast of the character of Pamina and Papageno, Tamino and Monostatos, the high priest Sarastro, and the masterly instrumentation, makes us entirely forget the sameness of time, As a most excellent example of an effective, carefully planned, and marvellously fine composed Finale we would also mention the Finale of the third act in Rossini's "Guillaume Tell," containing the meeting of the Swiss on the Rütli, when taking the oath to deliver their country from the invader.

THE FRENCH OPÉRA COMIQUE.

The chief qualities that distinguish French operas are grace, great clearness, a decided charm of rhythmical life and expression, and a considerable variety of happily conceived harmonious changes; also an undeniable elegance, a never-failing taste; also a peculiarly French quality, best defined as *piquancy*, or the power of *exciting* and maintaining the attention. In the French Opéra Comique the hostess is *Thalia*, the muse of Comedy, who invites as her guest *Euterpe*, the muse of harmony. The dialogue in the French Opéra Comique is an essential part of the whole, and even operas with an earnest story are interspersed with dialogue. In the French Opéra Comique *music* forms the smaller, and *dialogue* the larger ingredient; the story of an opéra comique is sometimes very intricate and complicated; and the process of developing the plot and bringing it to a climax could not be so intelligibly rendered by means of music, as through the words. Each scene must be full of humorous, witty, and spirited dialogues; and the libretto-writer is careful to provide interest and amusement to the spectators at every opportunity. ("Fra Diavolo," "La Part du Diable," "Le Brasseur de Preston," etc.) The performers are for this reason mostly very excellent actors; and the French public would consider a rich and powerful voice in an opéra comique not only superfluous, but actually a disturbing element, inappropriate and misplaced. But they deem, on the other hand, a graceful delivery, tasteful and precise variation of light and shade, and refined and correct enunciation—the "speaking expression"—indispensable qualities. The French Opéra Comique, therefore, possesses two important qualities—pliancy and subordination to the plot. In the Opéra Comique the music has to wait patiently till it receives its cue, and is allowed to appear, and even then it has to accommodate itself to the character of the preceding spoken passage; an undue desire to display independence could here not be admitted.

LITERATURE.—Dupuy, "Lettres sur l'origine et les progrès de l'opéra en France;" A la Haye, 1740. Grimm (F. M. von), "Almanac historique," etc.; Paris; chez Duchesne, 1752-1754, 4 vols. Noinville (Bernard de), "Histoire du Théâtre de l'Académie royale de Musique en France;" Paris, 1752. Reichardt (Johann Friedr.), "An das musikalische Publikum;" Hamburg, 1787. "Almanac des Spectacles pour l'année, 1856." Jahn (Otto), "W. A. Mozart," vol. ii. pp. 190, 203, 208, 241-256.

THE ITALIAN OPERA.

Italian operatic music may boast pre-eminence in many points, in which French and German music are deficient. The Italian melodies possess a thoroughly vocal construction; they also possess a broad and easy flow. Italian music is fresh and vigorous, and the pieces are constructed with clearness and precision. The voice part is nowhere interfered with or oppressed by the orchestra It rises, so to say, triumphantly above the accompaniment. The Italian "opera buffa" (comic opera) does not admit of dialogue; the so called "Recitativo secco" (see this form) is the connecting link that binds one air to another; the action of the opera buffa is always simple, transparent, sometimes even exceedingly poor and meagre. (See "Barbiere di Siviglia," "L'Elisire d'Amore," etc.) The criterion of the competency of the performers is not their power of acting, but entirely their vocal skill. The Italian composers of all times have recognized the necessity of consulting the compass, nature, and specialty of the human voice. But this admiration for the mere voice led the Italians too far. As soon as the so-called "Aria di bravura" had been invented, the supremacy of the singers over instrumentalists was declared; and it may safely be asserted, that where singers are the judges and umpires, the beauty, truth and dignity of the art are in danger. All great composers have complained that they are compelled to sacrifice dramatic truth, correct rules, and the unity of their works, merely to please the whims of singers, who do not in the least care for the musical work as such, and consider it simply as a vehicle for showing their own cleverness as executants. The spirit of the purely Italian opera music is more a natural than an intellectual one; the opera is in Italy considered a spontaneous and passing pleasure whilst the more earnest Germans look upon it as a serious art. "The Germans begin generally with *instrumental* music, which renders it difficult for them to subject themselves later to the conditions of vocal *music;* they find it not easy to become *simple*, whilst it is difficult for the Italians not to become *trivi*'." ("Rossini's Conversations with Hiller.")

LITERATURE.—Brown (John), "Letters on the Poetry and Music of the Italian Opera;" London, 1789. Mount Edgcumbe (Earl of), "Musical Reminiscences," etc.; London: Clarke, 1828. Rubbi (Andrea), "Il bello armonico teatrale;" Venezia, 1792. Finck (G. W.), "Wesen und Geschichte der Oper;" Leipzig: Wigand, 1838. Hogarth (George), "Memoirs of the Musical Drama;" London, 1838. Edwards (Sutherland), "History of the Opera;" vol. i. pp. 104, 140, vol. ii. pp. 80, 140, 226; London, 1862. Jahn (Otto), "W. A. Mozart," vol. i. pp. 343, 346, 349, 358.

GERMAN (ROMANTIC) OPERA.

Although German composers have written excellent comic operas (John Adam Hiller, Dittersdorf, Schenk, Müller, Kauer), and may boast of a good many distinguished lyrical and serious operas, the *Romantic* Opera seems to be the most sympathetic to the nature and feeling of the German composer and the German public. Among the authors who excelled in this branch of the dramatic art, we name more particularly Ludwig Spohr ("Faust," "Jessonda," "Alchymist"), Carl Maria von Weber ("Der Freischütz," "Oberon," "Euryanthe"), Heinrich Marschner ("Vampyre," "Hans Heiling"), and the lately deceased Richard Wagner ("Tannhäuser," "Flying Dutchman," etc.). The subject of the romantic opera is generally based on events of the fairy or supernatural world, or depicts the conflict of the evil and moral principle. The Romantic Opera draws also largely on the resources of the national myths and tales, paints with national colors, mixes original with national melodies, relies on the manifold means of the orchestra to describe, heighten, and complete certain dramatic situations, and finally admits the chorus for active co-operation. As in the Romantic Opera the characteristic expression is the principal one, it results that the composer's fancy is here more active and inventive than in other operas, which intend to show off the executive skill of the singers—indeed, the Romantic Opera contains more real music, and possesses, therefore, greater interest than operas which rely merely on pretty melodies, tuneful ballads, or brilliant vocalization.

ENGLISH (BALLAD) OPERA.

At all times the English public liked the introduction of ballads or songs in their operas. (See, for example, the celebrated "Beggars' Opera," with sixty-nine songs, and its second part, "Polly," with seventy-one songs (Dr. Chrysander's "Life of Handel," vol. ii. pp. 190-207). In this respect the English Opera resembles the early French operettas. Dramatic life and glowing warmth are generally wanting, and even in the present time the most gifted English composers have to suffer from this inartistic predilection of the public for ballads, which have at times to be introduced in direct juxtaposition to the dramatic requirements of the story. But not only the public is here to blame—part of the fault lies with the publishers, who would not think of publishing an opera without its containing half a dozen ballads. Many examples of correct dramatic feeling in English composers could be cited; although it is certain that the very works which contain dramatic life have never enjoyed that popularity which was reserved for so-called Ballad-Operas. The ballad of the English Opera is a lyric form, whilst the Opera as a dramatic form requires absolutely a greater, more intensive, and fiery expression, and must sometimes dispense with pieces of a distinct, concise form.

The form of the Opera being one of the most important, it will not be uninteresting to glance over a chronological table of the most celebrated composers of operas. (See pp. 100–103.)

INTERMEDIUM, INTERMEZZO.

Originally musical compositions interpolated in the comedies acted at court festivities, to amuse the spectators while the performers were resting or changing their dresses. Among the Italians they were already prevalent in the last quarter of the sixteenth century; they consisted both of *vocal* and *instrumental* pieces, the former being *madrigals*, with a varying number of voices and *dialoghi* for two or more choruses; the latter, symphonies, short passages imitating the madrigal in form. The vocal passages were, moreover, accompanied by instruments, the madrigals of one chorus by a *small*, and those of more choruses and the dialoghi by a *full* band. Afterwards this form was greatly elaborated by the addition of arias, duets, recitatives, etc., so that the interludes became dramatic works, consisting of musical scenes, mingled with dancing, and generally of a comic and farcial nature, even where associated with serious or tragic opera. These interludes were introduced with anything but an artistic or congenial effect between the acts of some of Molière's comedies, as performed before the Court of Louis XIV. For the last century this form has entirely fallen into desuetude, for it could not fail to be observed how absurdly the action of a work was interrupted by thus interweaving a form which had no relation to the main subject, and, indeed, was sometimes in contradiction with it.

In modern instrumental music a short movement introduced between two longer ones is often designated as an *intermezzo*. (See Mendelssohn's music to "A Midsummer Night's Dream," his String Quartets and Lachner's Suite in E.)

CHRONOLOGICAL TABLE OF THE MOST

	ITALY.		FRANCE.
	1550 (about) Cavalieri, Emilio del. 1560 (about) Peri, Giacomo. 1565–1649 Monteverde, Claudio. **1580 Invention of the Opera.**		
1600	1600–1670 Manelli, Francesco. 1600 (about) Gasparini, Michel Angelo. 1600–1662 Marazzoli, Marco. 1610– ? Cavalli, Francesco. 1610–1650 Sacrati, Paolo. 1610–1670 Ziani, Pietro Andrea. 1620– ? Rovetta, called Rovettino. 1620–1681 Cesti, Marc Antonio. 1625–1692 Legrenzi, Giovanni. 1633–1687 **LULLY**, Giovanni Battista (19 French Operas). 1640– ? Gabrieli, Domenico. 1640–1710 Zanetti, Antonio. 1645–1678 Stradella, Alessandro.	1600	1617– ? Cambert, Robert. 1635– ? Philidor, Michel-Danican. 1639–1709 Colasse, Pascal. 1645 *Introduction of the Italian Opera through Cardinal Mazarin.*
1650	1650–1730 Steffani, Agostino (Gregorio Piva). 1650–1720 Ziani, Marco Andrea. 1659–1725 **SCARLATTI**, Alessandro (115 Operas). 1665–1740 Lotti, Antonio. 1670–1743 Vivaldi, Antonio. 1672–1750 **BONONCINI**, Giovanni. 1678–1763 Caldara, Antonio. 1681–1736 Astorga, Emanuele. 1687–1767 **PORPORA**, Nicolo. 1694–1756 Leo, Leonardo. (*The first greater Overtures.*)	1650	1660 *The first French Opera.* 1662–1741 Desmarets, Henri. 1672 *Lully's first French grand Opera.* 1683–1764 **RAMEAU**, Jean-Philippe. *Great progress in the French Opera.*
1700	1703–1785 Galuppi, Baldassaro. 1706–1772 Lampugnani, Giovanni. 1707–1739 Pergolesi (Jesi), Giovanni Battista. 1711–1778 Perez, Davide. 1712–1795 Paradies, Pietro Domenico. 1714–1774 Jomelli, Nicolo. 1715–1787 Fiorillo, Ignazio. 1728–1800 **PICCINI**, Nicolo (130 Operas). 1730–1802 Sarti, Giuseppe. 1735–1786 Sacchini, Antonio Maria, Giuseppe. 1741–1816 **PAISIELLO**, Giovanni (94 Operas).	1700	1711–1773 Mondonville, Jean-Joseph. 1712–1778 Rousseau, Jean-Jacques. 1727–1795 **PHILIDOR**, François-André. (French and Italian Operas). 1727–1780 Berton, Pierre. 1729–1817 **MONSIGNY**, Pierre-Alexandre. 1733–1829 Gossec, François-Joseph 1741–1813 **GRETRY**, André-Erneste (59 Operas).

CELEBRATED COMPOSERS OF OPERAS.

	GERMANY.		GREAT BRITAIN.
1600	1585-1672 Schütz, Heinrich von (Sagittarius).	**1600**	
	1627 *Performance of the first German Opera (by Schütz).*		1620 (about) Eccles, John (Rinaldo e Armida, etc.).
			1620-1677 Lock, Matthias (Psyche, 1675).
	1640-1700 Strunk, Nicholaus Adam.		
	1641-1688 Franck, Johann Wolfgang.		
	1646-1725 Krieger, Adam.		
1650	1660-1732 Fux, Johann Joseph (17 Italian Operas).	**1650**	1658-1695 **PURCELL**, Henry.
	1673-1739 **KEISER**, Reinhard (116 Operas, 75 still known).		1665 (about) Clayton, Thomas (*Arsinoe, the first English Opera*).
	1681-1764 Mattheson, Johann (German and Italian Operas).		
	1681-1767 Telemann, Georg Philip.		
	1685-1759 **HANDEL**, Georg Friedrich (8 German and 43 Italian Operas).		
	1699-1783 **HASSE**, Johann Adolf (51 Italian Operas).		
1700	1701-1759 Graun, Carl Heinrich (30 Italian Operas).	**1700**	
	1714-1790 Holzbauer, Ignaz.		1710-1778 **ARNE**, Thomas Augustine (23 English Operas).
	1714-1787 **GLUCK**, Christoph Willibald (8 Italian and 13 French Operas).		
	1721-1795 Benda, Georg.		
	1728-1809 Hiller, Johann Adam.		
	1729-1774 Gassmann, Florian Leopold (23 Italian Operas).		
	1732-1809 **HAYDN**, Joseph (10 German and 14 Italian Operas).		
	1735-1782 Bach, Johann Christian (15 Italian Operas.)		1735-1795 Linley, Thomas.
			1737-1814 Dibdin, Charles.
	1739-1799 **DITTERSDORF**, Carl von.		1740-1802 Arnold, Samuel (40 English Operas and Operettas.)
	1749-1814 Vogler, Abbé Georg Joseph.		1746-1827 Hook, James (11 English Operas).

Chronological Table—(Continued).

	ITALY.		FRANCE.
1750	1750-1825 Salieri, Antonio (41 Operas).	1750	
	1752-1837 Zingarelli, Nicolo.		1753-1809 **DALAYRAC**, Nicolas (56 Operas).
	1754-1801 **CIMAROSA** (Domenico, 75 Operas).		
	1756-1812 Righini, Vincenzo.		
	1760-1842 **CHERUBINI**, Luigi (29 Operas, French and Italian).		
	1763-1845 Mayer, Simon (77 Italian Operas).		1761-1825 Gaveaux, Pierre.
	1767-1837 FIORAVANTI, Valentino.		1763-1817 **MEHUL**, Etienne Henri (42 Operas).
	1769-1832 Asioli, Bonifazio.		1766-1831 Kreutzer, Rodolphe.
	1771-1839 **PAER**, Ferdinando (51 Operas).		1767-1844 Berton, Henri Montan.
	1775-1818 **ISOUARD**, Nicolo (42 French Operas).		1768-1853 Jadin, Louis Emanuel.
	1775-1832 Garcia, Manuel (Spaniard).		1775-1834 **BOIELDIEU**, François Adrien (23 Operas).
	1778-? Puccita, Vincenzo.		
	1784-1841 Morlacchi, Francesco.		
	1784-1851 **SPONTINI**, Gasparo (16 Italian, 7 French and 3 German Operas).		
	1785-1849 Carafa, Michele (Italian and French Operas).		
	1791-1849 Vaccaj, Nicolo.		1789-1870 **AUBER**, François Daniel.
	1792-1868 **ROSSINI**, Gioachino (36 Italian and 4 French Operas).		1789-1861 Chelard, André Hyppolite.
	1796-? Pacini, Giovanni.		1791-1833 **HEROLD**, Louis.
	1797-1848 **DONIZETTI**, Gaetano (70 Italian and several French Operas).		1794-1841 Monpou, Hyppolite.
	1798-1870 **MERCADANTE**, Saverio.		1799-1862 **HALEVY**, Jacques.
1800	1802-1835 **BELLINI**, Vincenzo.	1800	1803-1856 **ADAM**, Adolphe.
	1804-? Gabussi, Vincenzo.		1808-1866 Clapisson, Antonin Louis.
	1809-? Ricci, Federigo.		
	1814- **VERDI**, Giuseppe.		1811- **THOMAS**, Ambroise.
			1818- **GOUNOD**, Charles François.
			1822-1884 Massé, Victor.

Chronological Table—(Continued).

	GERMANY.		GREAT BRITAIN.
1750	1751–1831 Kauer, Ferdinand (200 popular [Volks] Operas). 1752–1814 Reichardt, Johann Friedrich. 1755–1825 WINTER, Peter von. 1756–1791 **MOZART**, Wolfgang Amadeus (6 great Italian and 2 German Operas). 1756–1808 Wranitzky, Paul. 1760–1802 Zumsteg, Johann Rudolph. 1761–1836 SCHENK, Johann. 1763–1850 Gyrowetz, Adalbert. 1764–1823 Steibelt, Daniel (4 French Operas). 1765–1814 Himmel, Friedrich (4 Italian and 4 German Operas). 1766–1846 WEIGL, Joseph. 1767–1835 Müller, Wenzel (about 200 popular Operas). 1770–1827 **BEETHOVEN**, Ludwig van. 1782–1849 KREUTZER, Conradin (24 German Operas). 1783–1859 **SPOHR**, Ludwig. 1786–1826 **WEBER**, Carl Maria von (8 German Operas). 1794–1864 **MEYERBEER**, Jacob (5 French and 9 Italian Operas). 1795–1861 MARSCHNER, Heinrich. 1797–1828 SCHUBERT, Franz. 1798–1859 Reissiger, Carl.	1750	1750–1829 Shield, William (16 comic English Operas). 1757–1830 (?) Reeve, William (21 English Operas). 1763–1796 Storace, Stephen (14 English Operas). 1767–1838 Attwood, Thomas (about 7 Operas). 1767–1844 Mazzinghi, Joseph. 1774–1824 Davy, John (11 English Operas.) 1782–1855 **BISHOP**, Henry Rowley (63 English Operas).
1800	1803–1851 LORTZING, Carl. 1804– Lachner, Franz. 1804– Benedict, Julius. 1809–1849 Nicolai, Otto. 1811– Hiller, Ferdinand. 1812–1883 Flotow, Friedrich von (French and German Operas). 1813–1883 **WAGNER**, Richard. 1829– Rubinstein, Anton. 1838– Bruch, Max.	1800	1802– **BARNETT**, John. 1808–1870 **BALFE**, Michael William (Italian, French and English Operas). 1813– **MACFARREN**, Sir George. 1818–1865 **WALLACE**, Vincent (about 6 English Operas). 1842– **SULLIVAN**, Sir Arthur Seymour. 1847– **MACKENZIE**, A. C. 1852– **STANFORD**, Charles V.

INSTRUMENTAL MUSIC.

INSTRUMENTAL music is one of the most important and influential branches of the musical art; and has been the means of raising music as an art to that high pitch of excellence it has attained, and by virtue of which it need not fear comparison with any other art, whether poetry, painting, drama, or sculpture. No other art indeed is so thorough and complete a boon to all classes of society. The rest require education before they can be enjoyed. Sculpture, for instance, is a delight for the higher and better educated classes, whilst it will be more or less unintelligible, and therefore uninteresting, to the laborer and handicraftsman. Music, however, appeals directly to every class; the soldier, the forester, the sailor, the schoolboy, each and all delight in music.

> Nought so stockish, hard, and full of rage,
> But music for the time doth change his nature;—
> The man that hath no music in himself,
> Nor is not moved with concord of sweet sounds,
> Is fit for treasons, stratagems and spoils:
> * * * * * * * *
> Let no such man be trusted.

Some people have affected to consider music as a secondary art, and have asserted that it requires natural feeling, but not intelligence; but, on the contrary, instrumental music is one of the greatest triumphs of human intelligence. To construct, from isolated sounds, a sonata or symphony, to infuse into the work that irresistible energy and interest which compel a large audience to listen as if spellbound—this certainly requires a high degree of intellectual power in the musician. Vocal music is in so far the direct expression of our feeling, as it is uttered by the human voice, and thus has a close analogy with ordinary speech. Instrumental music expresses our feelings in an indirect way; it has to avail itself of a mechanical contrivance; the intended expression must be evoked from the lifeless instrument. Any one can sing who has a voice; to produce music from an instrument, a certain amount of skill is required. The singer expresses the feeling by soft or passionate tones; the instrumentalist tries to produce the effect by a sometimes involved combination of figures, rhythm, or harmonies. Besides, he is compelled to describe—as it were to portray—to use all possible means *indirectly* to produce an effect which is given in a direct and immediate manner by the voice.

Thus the domain of the voice is chiefly the expression of *sentiment*, whilst the instrument works in the domain of *fancy*. Vocal music, wedded as it is to words which to a great extent already give the sense of the piece, is more easily understood than instrumental music, which has to depend solely on the power and faculty of the composer to express his feeling and meaning in the most correct and comprehensible manner by musical tones. It is only in classical works that we find vocal music supplemented and its effects heightened by fancy;

and only in the best specimens of instrumental music does the composer's fancy manifest itself in almost articulate expression of feeling. Fancy and feeling go naturally together, and indeed ought to be united; but such union is rare, and is one of the surest signs of true genius. One of the principal conditions of instrumental music is the adherence, or we might say submission, to firm and rigorous rules. If instrumental music is not founded on a solid basis—if, so to say, the outlines of the building are not discernible to our mental view—if order does not reign throughout—if the composer's fancy is not disciplined, purified, and sobered by being confined within strict and precise limits—an instrumental piece will be little more than an incoherent mass of sounds, a kind of musical chaos.

When we consider all these indispensable conditions, and think of the simple material—namely, sound—out of which such masterpieces as the sonatas, quartets, and symphonies of Haydn, Mozart and Beethoven are constructed, we cannot withhold our tribute of involuntary admiration and amazement at the grandeur of the genius of these men. It is a common remark that to genius everything is accessible and possible, but it may be doubted whether the greatest genius is equal to the task of composing a quartet or a sonata without the closest and deepest study. It seems as if it were an easy thing to write such quartets as those of Haydn or Mozart, to construct such sonatas as those of Beethoven. But why does the achievement seem so easy? For the simple reason that in these works all rules, all laws, all conditions have been strictly fulfilled; the works themselves are so thoroughly suffused with the individual feeling of the composer, that absolute perfection is the result; and absolute perfection ceases to excite wonder, because the hearer's mind is not occupied with defects, and thus a part of the reasoning and critical faculty is not brought into action. In such a work the composer has brought his individual feeling so entirely into harmony with the object he had in view, that an equilibrium is produced which fills the hearer's mind with complete satisfaction.

But how were these great composers enabled to lay down such rules?—to decree these laws of beauty, of symmetry, of plastic grace—and to infuse into their works such a wonderful life? First of all they felt instinctively that it was indispensable to study the human heart, and to appreciate the different degrees of feeling produced by various phases of mental disposition. If, for instance, a person is melancholy, this state of feeling will not always be present in the same strength; a brighter moment may intervene, just as a ray of sun sometimes breaks through the cloud. The reaction, indeed, will intensify the feeling of melancholy; there will be all the more gloom after the bright moment, just as the dark cloud will appear thicker in its blackness after the cheering sunbeam which pierced it for a moment has disappeared. But contrast there must be;—and Nature herself shows us contrast in every possible phase. This necessity of contrast was clearly recognized by composers, and is musically produced by the different characters of the respective subjects or themes, and by their judicious distribution throughout the movement.

Again, if a piece consists of two, three, or four movements, it is essentially necessary to arrange those various movements in such a manner that a melancholy sentiment is relieved by a brighter tone; that an outburst of passion is succeeded by a feeling of calm; or that, on the other hand, a degree of passionate feeling, moderate at first, is gradually wrought up to the height of frenzy and despair.

Our great instrumental composers had to think deeply, and to exert the very highest intelligence, till they secured the characteristic and correct musical expression for their ideas. When they had selected the proper subjects for their work, they had still to collect all the necessary adjuncts for these subjects; they had to settle the proper figure, the accurate and fitting harmonization of the theme, the judicious introduction of episodes; they had to try whether a simple or a scientific treatment best suited the whole—indeed a great many points had to be considered and reconsidered—points which appear to the uninitiated only as natural consequences or accidental contingencies—and then only could the composer sit down and write a perfect and thoroughly effective work.

Whilst the composer of a song or an aria has merely to illustrate with sounds the subject provided for his fancy by the inventive genius of the poet, the instrumental composer must rely solely and entirely on his own inventive resources. He has to be both poet and musician. It is therefore evident that there is greater difficulty, and consequently greater merit, in composing a good quartet or symphony than in writing a good song.

Of a regular style of instrumental music we find no traces before A.D. 1500; and even then the province of the instruments was chiefly to play, as an accompaniment, the different voice-parts of the chorus; indeed almost all the different instruments were at that time in an undeveloped state, and only the organ was to a certain extent perfected. According to our most experienced historians, the first dance movements for instruments alone date from 1529, and were printed in Paris. When the recitative (which was preceded by the monody) was invented, it was of course necessary to accompany it with instruments; and we find that Carissimi in his cantatas introduced by degrees independent instrumental interludes and ritornelli. The same thing was done by Alessandro Scarlatti. Through the invention of the *stilo concertate* the stringed instruments were admitted into the church, where formerly only trumpets and trombones had been in use. About the end of the seventeenth, and particularly in the beginning of the eighteenth century, the labors of Corelli, Vivaldi, and Geminiani drew the general attention of the public towards instrumental music; the concerti grossi of Corelli, the violin concertos of Vivaldi, and different solos of Geminiani became highly popular; and by the invention of the suite, the forerunner of the sonata, instrumental music by degrees obtained an independent position.

With respect to the oldest forms of Instrumental music, it is necessary, in the first place, to mention the different names of the pieces and their respective meanings. We find preludes (voluntaries), toccatas, inventiones, ricercate, fugues, symphonies, intratas, concerti grossi, arias with doubles (variations), and suites and partitas.

PRELUDE.

(1) A piece which precedes a longer or more important movement, like the intrada or introduction to a symphony or sonata. The prelude or intrada which precedes an allegro movement is generally in slow, grave, and solemn time. (2) A prelude is more especially a

piece which precedes the choral; by such a prelude the organist may prepare the congregation for the choral to be sung, by using the entire melody of the choral or a part of it. (Compare Sebastian Bach's Choral-Vorspiele; see also Figured Choral.) (3) The prelude can also be used for public performances as a piece showing, like the etude, the technical skill of the executant; as such, the composer may use it as an independent piece, but generally the prelude is connected with a fugue. (See J. S. Bach's Forty-eight Preludes and Fugues; five preludes and fugues by Eberlin; Mendelssohn's Six Preludes and Fugues, Op. 35; Czerny's " Die Schule des Fugenspiels.")

In Sebastian Bach's Preludes and Fugues for the Organ we find the prelude treated in the same important manner as the fugue itself, and in some respects it here resembles the toccata. It is, however, very difficult to define exactly the difference between the toccata and prelude. The preludes of Chopin and Heller are merely little pieces, which have perhaps received this title for want of a better. The prelude is the only movement used in the suite which is not connected with the dance.

VOLUNTARY.

The Voluntary is an organ solo played before, during, or after any office of the church; hence it is called respectively introductory, middle, or concluding. Such solos were formerly, and are often still unpremeditated, or improvisations, as the name *voluntary* seems to imply. Clementi in his " Practical Harmony " gives the name Voluntaries to the five preludes of Eberlin.

TOCCATA.

The name Toccata is derived from the Italian *toccare*, " to touch." The toccata is a piece in which a certain passage or figure is repeated over and over again, either in the *strict* or the *free* style; in modern music the capriccio may be considered as the descendant of the ancient toccata. Organists generally selected the toccata as a means of showing their executive skill. The toccata has been greatly improved and enriched by Sebastian Bach, whose celebrated Organ Toccatas are not unlike fantasias. Robert Schumann has also composed an exceedingly clever toccata; and elegant and harmonious toccatas have been written by Clementi, Charles Meyer, Jos. Reinberger, Onslow, Czerny.

INVENTION.

Sebastian Bach gives this name to little rigorously written movements of two or three parts, which are rather ideas or inventions of the moment, than elaborate or seriously defined. The impromptu of modern times may be designated as an Invention.

RICERCATA.

The Ricercata (from Ital. *ricercare*—Fr. *rechercher*—" to seek ") is a piece which is not unlike a prelude. The executant tried in it to prepare the subjects to be treated afterwards in the principal piece, and so to invite the attention of the audience to the contents of the latter. Another meaning of the ricercata is, "a so-called master of art fugue (without episodes), in which all sorts of simple and double counterpoint, inverted movements, and *imitative*, technically called *canonical*, treatment of the single parts are contained." This sort of ricercata was considered a great test of intelligence and learning in an organist or composer. (Compare Ricercata, in Brossard's Lexicon.)

FUGUE.

(See Form with regard to the Relation of the separate parts of Polyphonic Music, p. 40.)

THE OLD SYMPHONY.

The word Symphony means a consonance or harmony of notes agreeable to the ear, whether the sounds be vocal or instrumental, or both. The English poets have used the word in the sense of consonance of sounds. Thus Gray's bard, hearing with prophetic prescience the harmonies of poetry that are to grace the Elizabethan era, exclaims:—

> What sounds symphonious tremble on my ear?
> What strains of vocal transport round me play?

The *Old Symphony* is a musical composition for a full band of instruments, and was synonymous with *Overture*. The performance of any one of the instrumental works already mentioned, such as the ricercate, fugues, etc., was also called a Symphony. The *Modern Symphony* has nothing in common with the old form but the sounding together of the different instruments. In this sense the symphonies of Sebastian Bach for the clavecin are also to be taken; these symphonies are merely pieces, in which three parts sound together.

INTRADE, INTRATA, INTRODUCTION.

Intrade, or *Entrada*, designates in the first place a short richly-scored instrumental piece, serving as an introductory movement to greater compositions of a secular style, and also used in the older operas instead of an overture. (See Symphony.) The Intrade consists properly of two repeated parts, but the word also designates instrumental introductions not confined to any particular form. But they have always a solemn, pathetic and awakening character, intended to excite the attention and interest for what is to come; this is seen, for instance, in the short introductions before the first allegro of modern symphonies. (See Mattheson, "Neu eröffnetes Orchester," p. 173; "Capellmeister," p. 233.)

Secondly, the name of Intrade is given to a kind of flourish (fanfare) of trumpets, accompanied by kettledrums.

Introductio, or *Introduzione*, is like the intrade, an introductory movement to greater compositions. In movement it is slow or moderate, and is likewise grave, and calculated to excite and arrest attention. Occasionally it is elaborated into the form of an overture, for the overture itself is sometimes called Introductio. In Mozart's "Il Flauto magico" the first movement of the opera itself, after the overture, is called Introductio.

CONCERTO GROSSO.

This form is best explained by a quotation from Dr. Chrysander's preface to Handel's Concerti Grossi: (The works of G. F. Handel, German Handel Society, part xxx.; Leipzig. Twelve grand concertos for violins, etc., in seven parts, composed by Mr. Handel.) "The part-books are designated violino primo concertino, violino secondo concerto, violino primo ripieno, violino secondo ripieno, viola, violoncello, basso continuo. These then are concertos for stringed instruments with a continuo for harpsichord accompaniment, and are set for an orchestra divided as was the old Italian orchestra, then almost universally employed, into a *concertino*, generally consisting of two violins and violoncello as solo instruments, and a *concerto grosso*, formed by all the rest of the orchestra fully manned. From the addition of this latter division the concertos of this kind took their name." (For further instruction see Dr. Chrysander's "Life of Handel," vol. iii. pp. 168–182,) The distribution of the movements is the following:—*Concerto I.* (1), a tempo giusto, C, allegro; (2), adagio, ¾, allegro (fugato), C; (3) allegro, ⅜. *Concerto VI.* (1) larghetto e affettuoso, ¾; (2) fugue, allegro ma non troppo; (3) musette, ⅔; (4) allegro, C; (5) allegro, ⅜ (a kind of scherzo).

It may therefore be seen that these concerti grossi are a kind of suite or partita for several solo instruments and orchestra. (Compare also the concerti grossi of Vivaldi, Corelli, and Geminiani.)

ARIA, WITH OR WITHOUT DOUBLES.

Mattheson in his "Der vollkommene Capellmeister" (p. 232) says: "Aria, with or without variations—which the Italians call *partite* and the French *doubles*—is composed for the clavecin or other instruments." The aria is generally a simple melody, consisting of two parts, so simple that it admits of all possible ornaments and treatments, which again allow the performer to show off his technical skill. The bass and harmonies are but rarely changed. (See Chaconne and Variations.)

In Sebastian Bach's Partitas, also in Suites of Mattheson, Handel, and others, the name of Air or Aria is given to a short movement of an expressive and melodious character. (See John Sebastian Bach's Partita, No. 4, in D major, and Handel's Suites Nos. 3, 5, 10, 14.)

GROUND.

(Fr. *Basse constrainte;* Ital. *Basso ostinato;* Ger. *Grund-Bass.*)

A passage of four or eight bars in length, constantly repeated, each successive time accompanied with a varied melody, harmony, or figure. (Compare Purcell's and Blow's Grounds; also Bach's Ciaccona for Violin, Passacaille in C minor for the Organ; Handel's Ciaccona with sixty-two Variations," etc.)

SUITE.

The name Suite is French, and means "a succession, or series of pieces." Before the sonatas attained to any degree of popularity, the pieces written for instruments were toccatas, fugues, fantasias, capriccios, arias with or without so-called doubles (variations). But more generally they were dances. Dance-tunes of all possible kinds, set for the spinet, harpsichord, clavichord, lute, viol di gamba and other instruments kept their place in the chamber, more particularly in France. When the dance-tunes were not used for dancing, they were worked out in greater dimensions and with greater care. Of the dance themselves only the characteristic type or expression was retained; for the tune was not immediately connected with the dance. The form and the number of bars could be increased, great attention was bestowed on the working out, counterpoint was used to consolidate and refine the part-writing, doubles or variations were introduced to give a certain elegance and brilliancy to the air—and thus the suite became the legitimate exponent of dance music. This office it retained for a long time; indeed the period before Haydn—the period of Kuhnau, Mattheson, Couperin, Rameau, Handel, Sebastian and Emanuel Bach, and Domenico Scarlatti—is intimately connected with the suite and its constituents, the old dance-tunes. The suite was brought to perfection by Bach and Handel, who managed to retain in these dance-tunes the real typical expression. The most popular old dances were the *Allemande, Bourrée, Brawl, Ciaccona, Courante, Gavotte, Gigue, Hornpipe, Minuet, Passacaglio, Passamezzo, Passepied, Polonaise, Rigadoon, Sarabande* and *Siciliano*. Generally all the pieces that constitute the suite are in the same key (a decided fault in so far as, notwithstanding the greatest variety and characteristic expression shown by the illustrious composers in the different movements, the sameness of the key must produce a certain monotony). The suite is composed either of dance movements only or is preceded by a præambulum. When the collection of pieces, generally called Suite, comprises other movements such as caprice, allegro, fugue, etc., the real name is—

PARTITA.

For the better understanding we place here, side by side, the contents of a suite and again that of a partita by John Sebastian Bach.

SUITE.	PARTITA.
(English Suite No. 1.)	(No. 2, C minor.)
1. Prelude.	1. Sinfonie.
2. Allemande.	2. Allemande.
3. Courante 1 and 2 with doubles (variations).	3. Courante.
	4. Sarabande.
4. Sarabande.	5. Rondeau.
5. Bourrée, 1 and 2.	6. Caprice.
6. Gigue.	

It will be observed that some of Handel's suites are actually partitas; for instance, we find in his Suite No. 3 the following pieces:—1. Prelude; 2. Fuga; 3. Allemande; 4. Courante; 5. Air with five Doubles or Variations; 6. Presto (founded on the Air). The suite was also called *Sonata di balletto* when it contained only dance movements, and *Sonata di camera* when it was constructed like the partita. Arcangelo Corelli, on the other hand, calls his suites Sonate da camera, and not Sonate di balletti. The suites or sonate di camera of Corelli are shorter than those of either Bach or Handel.

SONATA DI CAMERA (SUITE) BY CORELLI.

1. Largo. 2. Allemande. 3. Corrente. 4. Gavotta,
or
1. Allemande. 2. Corrente. 3. Giga.

It is difficult to state with any certainty the time at which the suite was invented; generally it is supposed that the first suites were written in France about 1650; in strictness the compositions of Dr. John Bull, Orlando Gibbons, and William Byrde, to be found in "Parthenia," are also suites. When the sonata was generally adopted, the suite as such fell into oblivion; although it may be said, that it reappeared in the divertimenti, cassazioni, serenades and notturnos. (See these forms.) The adaptation of the minuet in the sonata and symphony is decidedly a remnant of the suite. The suite has been re-established in modern music by Taubert, Lachner, Raff, Grimm and other composers. If we compare the suite with the sonata in form, we find that the latter is actually a condensed or shorter suite. The prelude or allemande of the suite is represented by the first movement of the sonata, the sarabande takes the place of the adagio, or andante, the gavotte or bourrée represents the scherzo and the gigue the finale. (See Dance-music.)

The best essay on the Suite has been written by Nottebohm, "Wiener Monatsschrift für Theater und Musik" (1855), pp. 408, 475; 1857, pp. 288, 340, 399. Compare also Brossard's Lexicon; Paris, 1703. Mattheson, "Kern melodischer Wissenschaft, 1737, p. 121, C. F. Becker, "Die Hausmusik in Deutschland," p. 29–32.

The modern forms of Instrumental music are divided into *cyclical* and *single* forms. The Cyclical form comprises a series of numbers, and under this head we find the sonata, trio, quartet, quintet, sestet, septuor, etc.; the symphony, cassazione, divertimento, serenade; also the concerto. In the category of Single forms we place the overture and all the smaller pieces, as notturnos, capriccios or scherzos, impromptus, ballads, reveries, barcaroles, and in fact all the innumerable trifles that crowd the music-publishers' catalogues.

I.

CYCLICAL FORMS.

SONATA.

The Sonata is by far the most important form, and may be considered the mainstay of instrumental music. Remarks on the technical construction of the sonata apply equally to the form of the trio, quartet, or symphony, which latter will therefore be treated in a somewhat shorter manner. The name Sonata is derived from the Italian verb *sonare*, "to sound," and is originally designated as a piece which has to be *played*, not *sung*. Prætorius in his "Syntagma musicum," published in 1614, says: "*Sonata, a sonando*, is thus called as it is not sung by human voices, but solely *sounded* by instruments." The old sonata, as we have it from Biber, Kuhnau, Mattheson, and others, contains the germs of the modern sonata, but not much more; it was rather to be considered as a shorter suite, in so far as the first movement had a great analogy with the allemande. The slower movement, again, has an affinity with the sarabande, and the last or quick movement with the gigue. Most of the old sonatas were composed for several instruments, generally stringed instruments and clavicembalo. The latter, the keyed instrument, was chiefly used for supplementing the whole with chords. In this style were the Twelve Sonatas for Violin, Bass, and Clavecin by Corelli, which appeared in 1683. Kuhnau, the predecessor of Sebastian Bach as choirmaster of St. Thomas's School, at Leipzig, consolidated this form. Domenico Scarlatti improved it in point of technical execution, but usually employed the form of one movement only. In the Six Sonatas of Francesco Durante, each work consists of two movements only, of which the first is called Studio, the second Divertimento. The Italian composers of the eighteenth century chiefly affected this form of two movements.

It was Emanuel Bach, the second son of the great Sebastian Bach, who fixed the present form of the sonata; even the greatest works of this kind by Beethoven are founded and built on Emanuel Bach's original plan. Joseph Haydn, an enthusiastic admirer of Emanuel Bach, improved the sonata to such an extent, that we could pass from Haydn's sonatas directly to those of Beethoven, without the intervention of Mozart's sonatas as a connecting link. Beethoven's sonatas were more influenced by Haydn's than by Mozart's. Among the modern sonatas those of Clementi, Dussek, Weber, Schubert, Schumann, Mendelssohn, and Brahms are most remarkable and highly influential works.

The modern sonata generally consists of three or four movements. The first movement determines its character, and the succeeding movements have to harmonize with the first, to heighten and to supplement its effect. The following is the design of the first movement. First part, chief or principal subject; transition into the second subject; after this the final group. This first part is generally repeated.

The second part consists of a thematic working out of both the first and second subjects; after which follows the so-called repetition, consisting of the principal subject, a short passage leading into the second subject; and then we have the coda, or summing up, with some concluding chords.

Sonata Form.

(First movement.)

	First Part.	Middle Part.	Repetition.
Order of subjects and their treatment.	Chief or principal subject, transition to second subject. Final group. Repeat.	Thematic working out or development of both the subjects of first part; called also the Free Fantasia, because unrestricted as to form.	Chief subject. Transition to second subject. Final group. Recollection. Finale.
Key.	Tonic. Modulation into the dominant or a related major key; or rarely, if the chief subject is in a minor key, to the minor key of the fifth above.	Free modulations return to the tonic.	Reign of the tonic.

It is evident that this form is liable, according to the length and character of the work, to certain modifications, chiefly affecting the working out of the principal subjects in the second part. The second movement is generally a largo, grave, adagio, or andante; and sometimes also an allegretto or moderato. It may appear either as a theme or a double theme with suitable variations; or in the form of a song or aria; or, lastly, in the sonata form, under which is understood that mentioned in speaking of the first movement. Another form of the adagio, but one very rarely applied, is that of the rondo, in which the principal subject recurs three or four times; an excellent specimen of this form is the slow movement of Beethoven's "Sonata pathétique." Owing to the slower time of the adagio or andante, its length, reckoned by bars, must be much shorter than that of the first movement. The chief aim of the composer in the adagio is to exhibit expression and feeling; the slow time precludes such a fine rhythmical design as is required for the first movement.

Form of Slow Movement in Beethoven's Op. 2, No. 1.

First Part.	Middle Part.	Repetition.
Chief or principal subject in F.	Subject in D minor. Transition to dominant of principal subject.	Chief subject in the form of a variation, recollection, coda, or finale.

Form of Slow Movement in Beethoven's (Sonata Pathétique), Op. 13.

First Part.	Middle Part.	Repetition.
Chief or principal subject in A♭ major. Transition into dominant. Return to chief subject. Variation. Tonic and dominant.	Subject in A♭ minor. Modulation to E major; and return to Tonic in the minor key.	Chief subject, variation. A short coda. Tonic.

The third movement is either a minuet or a scherzo. This form is exceedingly simple—it merely consists of two parts. The trio, which alternates with the scherzo or minuet, is constructed in the same manner. In some works of this kind, by Beethoven, Mendelssohn, and Schumann, the scherzo appears in the sonata form just described, and the place of the trio is here assigned to the second subject, a short working out, leading back to the principal theme.

Form of Scherzo or Minuet.

Scherzo or Minuet.		Trio.		Repetition.	
I.	II.	III.	IV.	I.	II.
Chief subject.	Development of chief subject.	Chief subject.	Development of chief subject.	Chief subject.	Development of chief subject.
Tonic.	Modulation, with close in tonic.	Related major or minor key.	Modulation, with close in tonic of trio.	Tonic.	Modulation, with close in tonic.

There are instances in which two trios are introduced. Examples of scherzi in the sonata form are Beethoven's Allegretto vivace in Op. 31, No. 3, his "Prestissimo" in Op. 199, and several scherzos in his String Quartets. See also Scherzo of Mendelssohn's Octett and Quintet, Op. 18; String Quartets, Op. 44, No, 2 in E, and No. 3 in E flat; Trios, Op. 49, 66, and others.

The fourth and last movement, generally called the finale, may appear in the following different forms: first, in the same form as described for the first movement:—

Form of Beethoven's Finale of Sonata No. 6.
(Op. 19, No. 2.)
(Sonata Form.)

First Part.	Middle Part.	Repetition.
Chief or principal subject. Transition to the second subject in the dominant.	Thematic working out or development of both the subjects of first part. Return to	Chief subject. Transition to second subject in the tonic. Short finale.

INSTRUMENTAL MUSIC.   115

Secondly, as a theme with variations:—

(See for example Haydn's Sonata in A major, No. 26 of Breitkopf and Härtel's, No. 17 in Pauer's Edition; Beethoven's Sonata No. 30 (Op. 109); Beethoven's Sonata No. 32 (Op. 111).

Thirdly, as a *Rondo*:—

BEETHOVEN'S SONATA NO. 4.
(Op. 7.)

Chief or principal subject. Transition to second subject. Return to principal subject, slightly varied.	New subject in the related minor key; first and second part. Transition and return to	Chief or principal subject. Transition to second subject, now in the tonic. Recollection and finale.

The rondo form is the most generally used. The musical term Rondo is derived from the French poetry in which the first verse, after being followed by a second, is repeated. The Old English roundelay was somewhat analogous in form. (See Canson redonda.)

In the musical rondo the chief subject appears three or even four times.

Another rondo form employed by Beethoven in his Sonatas Nos. 1 and 2 is:—

No. 1.

Minor Key.	*Major Key.*	*Minor Key.*
Chief or principal subject. Transition to second subject in dominant.	New subject in striking contrast to chief subject. Return to	Chief subject. Second subject in tonic. Finale.

No. 2.

Major Key.	*Minor Key.*	*Major Key.*
Chief or principal subject. Transition to the second subject in dominant. Repetition of the first subject in tonic.	New subject in two parts. Transition and return to	Chief subject (variation). Repetition of second subject in the tonic. Coda. Modulations, partly recollection of chief subject. Close.

Mozart in his "Rondo alla Turca" employs the following form:—

Chief subject, A minor. Parts i. and ii.	Second subject, A major. Parts i. and ii. in F♯ minor. Part iii. A major. Repetition of Part ii. Repetition of Part i.	Chief subject, A minor. Parts i. and ii. Repetition of Part i. of second subject.	Coda in A major. New subject.

As most interesting and instructive examples may be mentioned: Mozart's Rondos in A minor (six-eight time) and D major (common time); Beethoven's Rondos in C and G major, also the Rondo à capriccio in G major (Op. 129); Hummel's Rondo in B minor (Op. 103); Haydn's Gipsy Rondo; Mendelssohn's Rondo capriccioso (Op. 14), etc.

Each movement of the sonata may be said to form a separate whole, but each possesses a connection with the other movements. A certain unity of feeling must pervade the whole. The principal or chief feeling may pass through several modifications, and appear stronger or weaker, yet will return to its first or primary state. It may also happen that very opposite feelings suddenly appear, and vanish without leaving any trace of their presence. Such contrasts have been exhibited, though sparingly, by our great composers; judged from a psychological point of view they considered them as extravagances or indications of a state of feeling decidedly morbid. Notwithstanding this, our most modern music relies greatly on such effects from which a judicious estimate may be made of the value of modern music as compared with our grand old classics.

As regards the characteristic expression of the movements in most sonatas, we shall find that the *first movement*, with its symmetrically planned and broadly designed form, presents the firm and solid basis on which is founded the whole subsequent formal and ideal development. The *slow movement* is intended to soften and to tranquilize the mind previously excited by the first movement, where passion is the leading characteristic feature. The adagio moderates and subdues this state of feeling; or it may lead the mind, through an expression of suffering and grief, to a certain consciousness of calm happiness; or again it may tend to prepare it, by a temporary lull and quietness, for a still greater and more intense exaltation. The *Minuet* or *Scherzo* stands between these great and striking contrasts, and prepares the mind for the finale. The scherzo, with its quaint humor, reconciles us to the darker and more passionate passages; wit and jest here find an appropriate expression, and the composer has a welcome opportunity to show that, besides sentiment and passion, he possesses also humor and a genial fund of joviality. For instance, after a first movement full of passion and power, it is pleasant to find in the adagio calm and tranquilizing strains: these are indeed a necessary preparation for the final struggle.

Again, a first movement may be so majestic or so pompous that a similar broad movement to follow would seem out of place, uncalled for, and contrary to taste: the scherzo or minuet will here again be welcome, as an intervening stage or moderator. It is the aim of the finale to develop in the highest degree the character indicated and initiated by the first movement.

Thus the sonata contains all the necessary material for a regular psychological structure; and the production of a really good sonata is by no means the result of mere chance or accident; the work must be founded and built up on logical principles. This system of rising and falling emotion, of alternate excitement and tranquility, is analogous to the construction of periods in writing, and similar to the course a good speaker would adopt to arouse and refresh the attention of his audience; although in respect to music everything takes broader and larger proportions. Though a single movement of a sonata may be considered perfect in point of form, it is imperfect with respect to its entirety, representing only a single phase of that intellectual life which it is the province of the sonata to express in sounds. Diversity of expression is indispensable, because it enables us to understand such a long work as a sonata. A single movement extended to the length of an entire sonata or symphony would be wearisome in the extreme, an infliction rather than a source of pleasure to the hearer. By a judiciously selected variety of characteristic expression, however, one movement comes in as a relief to another, and the attention is kept up; but for this very reason it is necessary that every single part should be finished artistically, rounded off, and expressed in the most strict and concise manner; for a really satisfactory clearness of the whole can only result from the completeness of sequence and contrast in the component parts. The lack of characteristic expression will also be felt as a sad drawback; music without character loses half its value.

In music, logical reasoning and logical consequences may not, and even should not be subject to such fixed rules as *general* logical reasoning. But logic in music originates in sentiment; while general logic is derived solely from the intellect, and the presence of sentiment, so far from assisting, would frustrate it. The composer can express in the different movements, throughout all possible gradations, the principal character with which this piece is imbued. He should here work as the sculptor does in forming his first model: all the numerous musical expressions, whether derived from harmony, melody, rhythm, science, dynamic treatment, are at his command; and his correct feeling and refined taste, his enthusiasm tempered by judgment, will here show to the best advantage. The masterpieces of Haydn, Mozart, and Beethoven astonish by their order, regularity, fluency, harmony, and roundness, and by their splendid development into full and complete growth out of the sometimes apparently unimportant germ. Those great masters, Haydn and Mozart perhaps unconsciously, but the philosophical Beethoven certainly not without premeditation, observed and followed out the laws of nature; and thus it is that their works appeal so directly and immediately to the heart. (See Thematic work.) The solo sonata treats the form in the freest manner, more individually than in the case of the quartet and symphony. This is quite natural, in so far as the two latter are performed by several persons, and consequently the composer works out his polyphonic subject from a general point of view.

The solo sonata is like a mirror, reflecting the innermost ideas and feelings which move the composer's heart; when these individual feelings, as in the works of our classic composers, are regulated and penetrated by deep study, by the observance of strict rules—which observance has become wholly instinctive in the composer—a work will be produced which is intelligible to every one. Certain passages may be more or less interesting to certain individuals; but there will surely be a charm for every one—and this is the real and true test of a classical work, that it is mainly and firmly founded on principles dictated by nature and aided by science.

The piano-forte, possessing as an instrument the greatest variety of resources, has naturally been selected as the favorite interpreter of our classic masters' thoughts. The piano adapts itself equally to homophonic and polyphonic treatment; it can effectually produce melody and harmony, it offers favorable means for the most complicated rhythmical combinations; in short, it can do justice to almost everything the composer desires to express. That the instrument itself greatly influences the composer's inventive and creative faculty is certain; the composer's idea accommodates itself quite naturally to the capabilities of the instrument. We perceive, for instance, that sonatas for the organ are conceived in a spirit quite different from that which regulates those for the piano; contrapuntal and fugal treatment are much more often to be found in organ than in pianoforte sonatas. Again, the violin solo sonatas lend themselves more freely to a melodious treatment. It is in this the musical art shows its great superiority above the other arts. It can unite different instruments for one and the same work, and thus the composer can present to his hearers an almost endless variety of combination. The numberless charms in the duet-sonatas, trios, and quartets of Mozart, Beethoven, Mendelssohn, Schumann, and many others, give evidence of the wealth, grandeur, and beauty of Music.

PLAN OF BEETHOVEN'S SONATA (OP. 53), COMMONLY CALLED "WALDSTEIN" SONATA.*

* Reduced by C. Czerny. See Antoine Reicha's (1770–1836) "Traité de haute Composition musicale," etc. Paris, 1824.

INSTRUMENTAL MUSIC. 119

This first movement, so great with respect to ideas and execution, consists, including the repetition of the first part, of 385 bars in common time, and although it has to be played in quick time, it is of considerable length—a length which it would not be advisable to overstep in a solo sonata. Not less important is the point that this movement is, in the original, one of the most brilliant, bright, and difficult; yet, if we play through the above plan in the correct time, we find its harmonious structure, from beginning to end, *pure, simple,* and noble—indeed, it might be adapted for a chorus of a sacred composition. On such dignified, solid, and noble foundation rest all the great works of Beethoven—and we cannot give a better advice to the student than to analyze (or rather *reduce*) other classical works in a similar manner, and to fill up such structure afterwards with different melodies and harmonies; thus he will soon recognize how great an importance our classical masters attached to the invention of proper subjects, and how much care they bestowed in finding for them the appropriate harmonies and modulations. The student will see how, in the above instance, the distinguished and important first subject occupies the attention through twenty-one bars; this attention is increased by the modulation (bars 18-21) into a higher tone. With one single chord (bar 22), which lies outside of the previous rhythmical order, Beethoven proceeds to the augmented sixth on C, thence to the dominant of E minor; on this chord a suitable cadenza prepares the entry of the beautiful, hymn-like second subject in E major; this remarkable subject originates (like so many other subjects of Beethoven) in the diatonic scale—

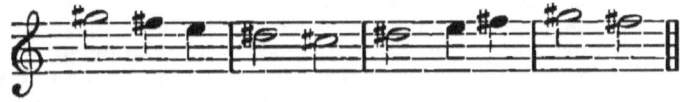

which, on its repetition, is surrounded by a graceful figure in triplets. Bars 50-58 bring a harmonious imitation, which, without any further or new modulations, leads to the final cadence; after which (bars 74-85) the modulation to E minor prepares, in a most natural manner, the return to the principal or first subject.

The construction of the second part is (bars 86-112) founded on the chief subject, and (in bars 112-141) on the imitation of the first part, everywhere appearing in a most interesting, yet natural harmonization, from bars 142 to 155, the return to the principal or first subject is prepared in a most effective manner. The first part, with the exception of a few interesting new points (bars 169-173), is merely repeated; the second subject appears now (bar 194) in A major (the sub-mediant). With bar 243 begins the final cadenza, which, after working out in a beautiful and highly interesting manner the principal subject, and after a brilliant final cadence and some tranquilizing recollections of the second subject (bars 282-292), closes the whole movement in a powerful, brilliant, and compact way.

The admirable unity and symmetry of the whole movement results from the following reasons: First, the movement is not crammed with too many different melodies or subjects; it possesses only four—the principal and second subject, the subsequent imitation and the final melody (see the original sonata, bars 74-85). Secondly, the choice of the different ideas is always happy, and they are connected with each other in a beautiful and entirely natural manner. Thirdly, the modulations are nowhere forced or strange, and always presented in a strict *rhythmical* order. Fourthly, each period has its appropriate length. Fifthly, the form is from beginning to end beautifully designed and faithfully executed.

LITERATURE.—Kuhnau (Johann), Preface to his "7 Partien und einer Sonate aus dem B" (B flat); Leipzig, 1696, 1710, and 1724. Becker (C. F.), "Die Hausmusik in Deutschland," pp. 33–39. Faisst (Imanuel), "Beiträge zur Geschichte des Clavier Sonate" (Cäcilia, vol. xxv. p. 132, Schott and Co.). Elterlein, "Beethoven's Clavier Sonaten;" Leipzig; English translation by Miss E. Hill; London: Reeves. Mattheson (J.), "Neu-cröffnetes Orchester;" Hamburg, 1713, p. 175. Scheibe (Joh. Adolph), "Kritische Musikus;" Leipzig, 1745, 74, p. 675.

STRING QUARTET.

This form occupies a unique position in the gallery of musical creations. It is well known that the Quartet, though invented by an Italian, Luigi Boccherini (1740–1805), was greatly improved by Haydn, Mozart, and Beethoven. Every composer of note in German has thrown himself heart and soul into the composition of quartets; more pains and scrupulous care have been bestowed on the selection and refinement of the proper subjects for a quartet, and more energy and zeal have been displayed in the working out of the whole, than in the construction of many an opera. The quartet may be considered as the test of the genius, scholarship, taste, feeling, and readiness of the composer. (See Thematic work.) Consummate skill is required in handling the subject, the most polished taste and judgment in the selection of the proper themes, and the purest and most genuine feeling, to suffuse the whole with that moderate yet sufficient warmth necessary to excite and maintain true interest among the audience. And yet the quartet, as a form, is not so popular as, for instance, an opera; and the success of a work of this kind will never be so brilliant and dazzling as that of a dramatic work, which, appealing to a larger and more mixed audience, has a much greater chance of general approbation. The quartet will remain, at least for some time to come, "caviare to the general." Nevertheless, the success of the quartet rests on a more solid basis—on the sympathy and firm connection between the composer, the executants, and the public—a connection favored by and based on good and pure taste, solid studies, and an interchange of refined feeling and intelligence. It is in fact a delightful unanimity produced by good music, good execution, and an intelligent audience. There cannot exist a more genuine or legitimate pleasure than to listen attentively to a fine quartet well executed. As already indicated, the quartet, like the trio, quintet, sestet, etc., is composed in the regular sonata form.

To the same department belong the—

CASSAZIONE, SERENADE, DIVERTIMENTO, NOTTURNO.

The *Cassazione* was in Italy a very popular piece, consisting of an indefinite number of movements, intended for outdoor performance in the evening. The earliest cassazioni were nothing more than suites set for different instruments; but these various instruments were not treated as an orchestra, but as solo instruments. There exist three

INSTRUMENTAL MUSIC.   131

cassazioni by Mozart, of which the last two are written for two string-instruments (tenor and bass), two oboes, and two horns. The *Divertimento* (piece for diversion) is a similar composition. The single movements were not written in the rigorous style, but in an easy popular manner; and it was sometimes the fashion to give the preference to a solo instrument. Mozart wrote no less than eighteen divertimenti, of which one (that in D major) has been successfully performed in several towns in England. The *Serenade* is generally written for wind-instruments; in it the march, and still more the minuet, is a very prominent feature. Of Mozart we possess twelve serenades; also two by Beethoven. Johannes Brahms, one of the most distinguished of living composers, has also written two serenades for a small orchestra. The *Notturno* is the same as the Serenade. Spohr's Notturno in C (Op. 34) and Hummel's Notturno in F (Op. 99) have obtained great celebrity.

Plan of Mozart's Cassazione in G (composed 1768), Köchel's "Verzeichniss," 63, p. 74:—*Marcia* $\frac{2}{4}$, in G major; *Allegro*, C, in G major; *Andante*, $\frac{2}{4}$, in C major; *Minuet* (I) in G major; *Adagio*, C, in D major; *Minuet* (II) in G major; *Finale*, $\frac{6}{8}$, in G major. Seven movements.

Plan of Mozart's Serenade in D major (composed 1770), Köchel's "Verzeichniss," 100, p. 101:—*Allegro*, C, in D major; *Andante*, $\frac{2}{4}$, in D major; *Minuet* (I) in G major; *Allegro*, $\frac{2}{4}$, in D major; *Minuet* (II) in D major; *Andante*, $\frac{2}{4}$, in D major; *Minuet* (III) in D major; *Allegro*, $\frac{6}{8}$, in D major. Eight movements.

Plan of Mozart's Serenade in D major (composed 1776), Köchel's "Verzeichniss," 250, p. 219:—*Allegro maestoso*, C, in D major; *Andante*, $\frac{2}{4}$, in G major; *Minuet* (I) in G minor, with Trio in G major; *Rondo*, $\frac{2}{4}$, in G major; *Minuet* (galant) (II) in D major; Trio in D minor; *Andante*, $\frac{2}{4}$, in A major; *Minuet* (II) in D major; Trio (I) in G major; Trio (II) in D major; *Adagio*, C, in D major; and *Allegro assai*, $\frac{6}{8}$, in D major. Eight movements.

Plan of Beethoven's Serenade, Op. 8, in D major (composed 1797):—*Marcia*, C, in D major; *Adagio*, $\frac{2}{4}$, in D major; *Minuet*, in D major; *Adagio*, $\frac{2}{4}$, in D minor; *Allegretto alla Polacca*, $\frac{2}{4}$, in F major; *Tema con Variazioni*, $\frac{2}{4}$, in D major. Six movements.

Plan of Johannes Brahms' Serenade in A, Op. 19:—*Allegro*, ₵ A major; *Scherzo*, $\frac{2}{4}$, in C and Trio $\frac{3}{4}$ in F; *Adagio non troppo*, in A minor, $\frac{12}{8}$; *Quasi Menuetto* in D, $\frac{2}{4}$; Trio, F sharp minor, $\frac{2}{4}$; *Rondo* (*Allegro*), in A, $\frac{2}{4}$.

Plan of Mozart's Divertimento in E flat (composed 1777), Köchel's "Verzeichniss," 289, p. 247:—*Adagio*, $\frac{2}{4}$, and *Allegro*, C, in E flat; *Minuet*, in E flat; *Adagio*, $\frac{2}{4}$, in E flat; *Finale*, ₵, in E flat. Four movements.

Plan of Mozart's Divertimento in D major (composed 1779 or 1780) Köchel's "Verzeichniss," 334, p. 274:—*Allegro*, C, in D major; *Andante*, $\frac{2}{4}$, in D minor, with six variations; *Minuet* (I) in D major; *Adagio*, C, in A major; *Minuet* (II) in D major; *Rondo*, $\frac{6}{8}$, in D major. Six movements.

Plan of Spohr's Notturno in C major, Op. 34:—*Marcia*, C, in C major; *Menuetto*, $\frac{3}{4}$, C minor; *Andante con Variazioni*, C, in F major; *Polacca*, $\frac{3}{4}$, in C major; *Adagio*, $\frac{2}{4}$, in A flat major; *Finale*, $\frac{2}{4}$, in C major. Six movements.

We now pass to the highest form of instrumental music, namely the Symphony.

SYMPHONY.

All the remarks concerning the structure of the Sonata apply also to the *Symphony*. In the Symphony a certain number of instruments are united, to produce a poetical representation of a series of emotions of the soul. The emotion may be tragical, heroic, and grand, or light and humorous—provided only it possesses sufficient importance to be worthy of representation. Such importance is not only rendered necessary by the chorus-like composition of the orchestra itself, but also by the broader and grander treatment the symphony must have, to distinguish it from the sonata or quartet. A quartet, even if scored for all the instruments used in the symphony, will yet not be a symphony. A sonata or quartet may show symphonic ideas and be treated symphonically; but it could never be taken for a symphony, inasmuch as the symphony, written for a larger audience and for a large hall, addresses itself to a mixed audience, and must necessarily rely on a more general treatment and on a still clearer and more precise delineation of the component parts than are absolutely demanded for the sonata or the quartet. The presence of so many different instruments, each and all possessing a separate and individual expression and character, the combination of so many different tone-shades—in short, the richness of the whole material, offers to the composer a wide scope for describing in sounds a definite poetical subject. No better example of this style could be adduced than Beethoven's "Pastoral" or "Eroica" Symphony; but on the other hand all sorts of descriptions put forth by self-constituted annotators, and purporting to interpret movements, themes, chords, or passages in various symphonies, are not only in bad taste, but are sometimes simply ridiculous, and have often nothing whatever to do with the poetical idea in the composer's mind.

As poetry finds its fullest development in the *drama*, so does instrumental music in the *symphony;* and indeed it may safely be said that the symphony is the highest of all the musical forms, because it demands from the composer an extraordinary amount of power and originality, and an absolutely independent inspiration. The thematic subject must contain in itself the whole idea of the work; from it must be developed all the following logical consequences. But even the invention of an excellent principal subject, and one suitable for all purposes, would be an insufficient guarantee for a good symphony. Many more details have to be considered. A consummate mastery in handling counterpoint, instrumentation, invention of figures, appropriate interpolation of episodes, grouping of phrases, gradation of final effects, and a complete command over all these means, these various important details, is necessary before this greatest of instrumental forms can be satisfactorily constructed. When the architect has drawn the plan of a gorgeous-palace, he has many artisans to help him to carry out his idea; not so the composer of a symphony—he must be at once the architect, the builder, and decorator. No musical form, be it Opera, Oratorio, or any other, could give us that noble and lofty idea of the wealth and intrinsic power or of the irresistible strength of music that we find in the Symphony.

CONCERTO.

(Concerto di camera.)

The *Concerto* is a piece consisting of three movements, in which one particular instrument is regarded as the solo instrument and is accompanied by a small or larger orchestra. In modern times the Concerto is not reckoned as chamber-music, but belongs to the orchestral department. The Concerto di camera consists (like the more modern concertos of Haydn, Mozart, Beethoven, Moscheles, Field, Viotti, Spohr, Rode, etc.) of three movements, of which the first and last are quick, and the middle movement (andante, larghetto, adagio) slow. The form of the different movements is that of the Sonata, with the exception of the so-called *tutti* (ritornello, prelude, introduction), which is performed by the orchestra; this tutti contains generally both subjects, the principal and second one, and makes the movement much longer. For this reason Mendelssohn and Schumann have introduced most acceptable improvements, by reducing the orchestral prelude to the shortest dimension, and by intrusting to the principal instrument the disposition of the movement. In the older form, we have actually to traverse the same road twice over, and this plan results in making the performance of the solo or principal part a kind of variation. Although Mozart and Beethoven succeeded to impart by their genius sufficient interest to the tutti, and at the same time to elaborate and enrich the solo part with such charm and fascination as to make the listener forget that the solo part had already been heard once before, in a simpler manner; less richly gifted composers could not make the tutti or solos so interesting, and the result is therefore not very happy, indeed rather monotonous. The concertos of Mozart, Beethoven, Field, etc., introduce towards the end a kind of "free fantasia," generally called *Cadenza*. This cadenza offers to the executant a means of showing not only his skill as a performer, but also a test for his cleverness as a composer, in so far as there is in it a kind of "summing up" of the entire movement. This cadenza begins generally with the $^6_4$ chord on the dominant, and may be long or short. The cadenza of the last movement is generally shorter than that of the first movement. (See Beethoven's and Mozart's cadenzas to their own concertos; A. E. Müller's cadenzas to six of Mozart's concertos; also the cadenzas of Moscheles, Reinecke, and Rubinstein to concertos of Beethoven; various cadenzas, and most especially Schumann's splendid cadenza to his concerto, Op. 47, A minor.) The beauty of the concertos of Mozart and Beethoven consists in the interweaving of the orchestral instruments with the principal part; thus making it a kind of dialogue. According to Quantz, the celebrated flute-player and musical companion of Frederic the Great of Prussia, Giuseppe Torelli (1616-?1708), a famous violinist from Bologna was the founder of the concerto form, which was adopted by Franz Benda, Antonio Vivaldi, and others.

The structure of the Concerto might be thus explained:—

First Movement.

Tutti.	*Solo.*	*Solo.*
First or chief movement. Second subject sometimes in the tonic. *Solo.* Repetition of first and second subject. *Tutti.*	Thematic working and development of both subjects. Short tutti generally leading to the	Second subject in the tonic. Close in the tonic. Short tutti stopping with $^6_4$ chord on the dominant. *Cadenza.* Short tutti.

The slow movement is generally much shorter; and in many instances the romanza, barcarole, in short a lyrical form, is used.

The composer's intention is to show, in the slow movement, grace, elegance, tenderness, and suavity, as contrasted with the greater energy of the first movement and the hilarity or brilliancy of the last.

The *Finale* is mostly written in the six-eight or two-four time. If it is called Rondo, the form is that of a rondo in a sonata; but sometimes it receives also a characteristic expression, such as Rondo alla spagnuola (Hummel, Spohr), Rondo alla polacca (Beethoven, Op. 56), Rondo guerrière, and so on. No better examples of well-composed concertos could be mentioned than those of Mozart (twenty-two), Beethoven (Op. 15, 19, 37, 56, Triple Concerto, 58, 73), Spohr and Moscheles. The Fifth Concerto for Piano-forte, Op. 73, by Beethoven, is conceived in the manner of a symphony, and the Third Concerto, Op. 37, in C minor, belongs to the most perfect works of musical art —perfect with regard to the psychological correctness of development of feeling, the absolute perfection of formal beauty, the nobility and melodious beauty of the principal subjects, and finally, the richness of harmony and ever fascinating interest of instrumentation. The student is particularly advised to make himself thoroughly acquainted with the mutual relations of the principal instrument and the orchestra, which in this instance, as also in Beethoven's other concertos, is a real artistic triumph.

The double or triple concerto is constructed after the same manner; only that instead of *one* principal instrument the composer employs two, three, or four. The most celebrated examples of this form are Sebastian Bach's concerto for three clavecins, several of his concertos for two pianos, two violins; Mozart's concertos for violin and viola, for two piano-fortes, for flute and harp, Beethoven's concerto, Op. 56, for piano, violin and violoncello, Maurer's concerto for four violins, etc.

CONCERTINO, CONCERTSTÜCK.

Both these forms are smaller than that of the concerto; the tuttis and the development in the second part are much shorter, the slow movement is generally a romanza or a kind of song without words (see Mendelssohn, Op. 25, 40), and the last movement is at times a repetition of the first movement, or a rondo, or brilliant movement in the sonata form (see Mendelssohn's finales to his concertos, Op. 25, 40). Weber's Concertstück again is a kind of suite, consisting of four movements: (*a*) larghetto, (*b*) allegro passionata, (*c*) tempo di marcia, (*d*) piu moto leading into a presto assai.

The Concerto concludes the list of Cyclical forms belonging to instrumental music. We have now to speak of the overture, and afterwards of the minor forms which belong more or less to the domain of chamber-music.

OVERTURE.

This form may be divided into the old (French and Italian) and the modern overture. The composer Lully (1633-87), the founder of the French Opera, was also the inventor of the so-called *French Overture*. Its form consisted of a movement in common time, generally called the "grave" (solemn or heavy), followed by a fugue, which may be set in another key and in different time; after the fugue, part or whole of the grave is repeated. This form became so popular, that Handel, Bach, Keiser, Telemann, Hasse, and other composers of the eighteenth century adopted it. Where the overture was performed singly, and not in connection with the opera, it took in concerts the place of a symphony. The *Italian Overture*, as introduced by Alessandro Scarlatti, was quite different; it consisted of three distinct movements, the first and last of which were fast. The middle movement was scored for fewer instruments, and possessed a different character from the preceding and the following one. It was, in fact, in itself a kind of short symphony.

The modern overture may be divided into three classes: the *Opera Overture*, the *Artistic Overture*, and the *Concert* or *Programme Overture*. The Opera Overture has been perfected by Mozart, Weber, Spohr, and others with great attention and care; whilst the Italian and French composers did not bestow much attention on it. Thus with Rossini (the overture to "Guillaume Tell" excepted), with Boieldieu, Auber, Adam, Bellini, Donizetti, and others, the overture is nothing but a loosely connected string of the most popular airs which occur in the opera. Weber, in his overtures to "Euryanthe" "Der Freischütz," and "Oberon," followed the same plan, but arranged his airs with much greater care; moreover, his themes are so greatly superior to those of his Italian and French contemporaries, that his overtures are decidedly more important. Under the head of "Artistic Overtures" must be classed Mozart's overture to "Il Flauto Magico," Beethoven's great Overture in C major (Op. 124), Mendelssohn's overture to "St. Paul." Each of these is written in the style of a free fugue. The Concert or Programme Overture was initiated by Beethoven's "Coriolan," "Egmont," and "Leonora" overtures; and this field was also most successfully worked by Mendelssohn in his four grand concert overtures: the "Hebrides," "A Midsummer Night's Dream," "Fair Melusina," and "Calm Sea and Prosperous Voyage." The Concert Overture offers an excellent opportunity for tone-painting; its form is mostly that of the first movement of a sonata; its length is generally greater than that of the Opera Overture. The *Festival* or *Triumphal Overture*, another form less frequently followed, is generally written in the same manner. Musical literature is exceedingly rich in good, effective, and brilliant overtures; and their moderate length and mostly popular style render them great favorites with the general public.

PLAN OF OLDER OVERTURES.

OLD FRENCH OVERTURE (LULLY, etc.)

Grave.	*Fugue.*	*Grave.*
Very slow and solemn. Transition in the dominant or relative minor or major key.	Quicker movement.	Repetition (only partly) of first part, with slight variations of the chief subjects.

OLD ITALIAN OVERTURE (ALESSANDRO SCARLATTI).

First Movement.	*Second Movement.*	*Third Movement.*
Quick movement.	Slower time, also different from the time of the first movement, less richly scored.	Quick and brilliant.

PLAN OF HANDEL'S OVERTURE TO "THEODORA."

Maestoso.	Allegro.	Larghetto.	Courante.
Common time. G minor.	Fugue. Common time. G minor.	(Minuet.) E flat. Three-four time.	Three-four time. G minor.

PLAN OF HANDEL'S OVERTURE TO "SOLOMON."

Largo.	Allegro.	Allegro.
Common time.	Fugue. Common time.	Three-four time.

II.

SINGLE FORMS.

FANTASIA.

FIRST among the smaller forms stands the *Fantasia*. The fantasia is an immediate result of a sudden inspiration, and need not necessarily follow any fixed rules; although Bach, Handel, Mozart, Beethoven, Hummel, Moscheles, Mendelssohn, and Schumann could not help bringing strict order even into this free, independent, and until their time unrestricted, form. The classical fantasia depends on the original invention of the composer, whilst the more brilliant concert-fantasia is generally founded on national or operatic airs. Bach's Chromatic Fantasia, those of Mozart in C major and C minor, Beethoven's G minor (Op. 77) and Choral Fantasias (Op. 80), Mendelssohn's in F sharp minor (Op. 28), Schumann's in C (Op. 17), and Hummel's in E flat (Op. 18) are standard works of the highest value. The modern fantasias of Thalberg, Liszt, and others are more or less *potpourris* (mixed compositions), made up of various themes. Although they are a good vehicle for the display of technical brilliancy of execution and dashing and effective playing, they cannot claim any high value as compositions. A masterly fantasia is that of Moscheles on Irish airs.

CAPRICE.

The *Caprice* is a movement in which one particular subject is treated in every possible manner, so that it appears as if the composer were capriciously resolved not to let the subject go before he had completely exhausted its resources. The caprices of Müller (1767–1807) and Mendelssohn are, however, written in the sonata style.

CAPRICCIO (SCHERZO).

The *Capriccio* or *Scherzo* must not be confounded with the *Caprice*. Although initiated by Beethoven, it may be almost called an invention of Mendelssohn's; for in its construction all the qualities are absolutely required which made Mendelssohn famous—namely, wit and spirit, an almost electric rapidity of harmonious changes, and a fairylike lightness of treatment in the whole subject. A scherzo or capriccio ought to float as it were in the air, and should appear entirely ethereal; its whole essence is sport, jest, hilarity, and brightness. In Mendelssohn's different scherzos these characteristics are fully developed.

The *Scherzo* (see Sonata) was a natural consequence of the improvement which the sonata made with respect to its progress as a psychologically conceived and constructed form. The slow and somewhat heavy minuet could not satisfy any more the demands of the composer, and thus we see that particularly Beethoven gave to the scherzo soon the place of the minuet (see his Op. 29, 30, i.; 31, iii.; 55, 59, i.; 68, 69, 74, 92, 96, 106, 110). Thus we find in his sonatas, duet sonatas, trios, quartets, and symphonies a greater number of scherzos than of minuets. The scherzo was, however, already used by Sebastian Bach in his Partita III.; and the *burla* or *burlesca* of older composers is indeed very like the scherzo.

THE VARIATION.

The *Variation* as a form is really one of the greatest wonders of our musical art. It is based on the principle that an air may appear in various kinds of figure and rhythm, and in varied division and complication of parts, changes of harmony, with contrapuntal and even fugal treatment, provided the melodious order and phrasing is preserved throughout. The *form* changes, but the *substance* remains. But changes of form are not immaterial, for they involve changes in the movement, expression, and even character of the original theme, which should develop itself in ever new phases. Variations are not like a chain formed by links of the same size—they represent progress from simple to composite, from rest to motion, from tranquility to passion, or *vice versâ*. Variations may be treated as a mere plaything with passages and ornate phrases (variazioni di bravura; see such works by Kalkbrenner, Czerny, Herz, Hünten, Döhler), without the requisites just mentioned, from the great facilities there are for change; but we speak here of those of the highest class, and in this field the musical art may achieve the greatest triumphs.* The composer,

---

* The student is advised to examine with earnest attention the following set of Variations:—Sebastian Bach's Air with Thirty Variations in B flat; Handel's Air and Variations in D minor; Rameau's Gavotte and Variations in A minor; Haydn's Andante and Variations in F minor; Mozart's "Unser dummer Pöbel meint" and Duet Variations in G; Beethoven's Variations in E flat (Op. 35), Thirty-two Variations in C minor; Thirty-three Variations in C on Diabelli's Valse; Schubert's Duet Variations in A flat (Op. 35); Mendelssohn's Variations sérieuses in D minor; Variations (Op. 83) in B flat, and (Op. 82) in E flat—compare the transformation of Op. 83 into the Duet (Op. 83A); Schumann's Variations (Etudes symphoniques) in C sharp minor (Op. 13), and Andante and Variations for two Pianos (Op. 46); Brahms' Variations on Themes by Handel, Schumann and Paganini; V. Lachner's Forty-two Variations on the Scale of G major (Op. 42); Raff's Variations from Second Suite.

bound, so to say, to the theme, develops in it new features, elevates it to a higher standard, and elicits from it fresh and unexpected beauties. This faculty is an exclusive privilege of music, and is found in no other art. The only equivalent we would mention as approximating at all to the unique form of the musical Variation might perhaps be the "Essay," in which the author may ring the changes on his subject.

MARCH.

(Fr. *Marche*; Ger. *Marsch*; Ital. *Marcia*.)

The March is of German origin, and dates from about 200 years ago. Well-defined rhythm is the characteristic quality necessary for its purpose. The utility of the march in encouraging wearied men to resist fatigue and inspiring them to advance against the enemy has been abundantly proved. Certain marches played by the military bands are said to have had no small effect in insuring victory. There are *three* great divisions of the march—namely, the *quick* march (Geschwind-marsch, Pas accelleré) the *slow* march, and the *funeral* march (Trauer-marsch, Marche funèbre, Marcia funèbre).

1. *The Quick March.*—This is used at the march-past of the soldiers and in the ordinary march-out. It is indispensable that the time fitted to the step (one, two, one, two) should be strongly accentuated; two-four time is the best, and a quaver and a quaver rest is the simplest form—

but the bar may be broken up to prevent monotony. Where a more flowing figure is employed, the accompaniment must strongly mark the rhythm; the first bars should be in the strict style. In the ordinary march, which is intended to exhilarate the soldier, the six-eight time and the alla breve (₵) time are often used; even the march-past is now less stiff than formerly. A military march must be brief; in the part of each instrument ten bars to a line of music and eight lines to the whole march should be the limit. The march generally consists of two distinct parts; the first number is sometimes called the *Initial March*, the second is the *Trio;* They are generally tolerably equal in length.

1. *Initial March.* First Part (8 bars).

Second Part (8 bars).

For variety's sake a different combination from that of the initial march is adopted in the trio. The trio is sometimes written in the key of the sub-dominant, and in it the melodic figure is greatly expanded; the second part of the trio begins in the minor key corresponding to the major key of the initial part, which is played as a termination after the trio, that the march may conclude in the key in which it began. The march is generally preceded by four or eight preparatory bars :—

2. *The Slow March.*—Mandel, in his "System of Music," p. 355, remarks that the slow march is retained in no European army, except in the English, which he considers a loss from a musical point of view." In England it is used for the march-past and for trooping the colors. Like the quick march it must not be too long; it is also divided into the initial and trio. An elaborate march of this kind might be mentioned—Mendelssohn's "Wedding March." The march called the "Troop," and used for trooping the colors is combined of nine marches, slow and quick; the "British Grenadiers" and "God save the Queen" being indispensable elements.

3. *The Funeral March*—the *Marcia lugubre* of the Italians, *March funèbre* of the French, *Trauer-marsch* of the German ($\quarternote = 66$) sixty-six crotchets to a minute by the metronome.—The initial is generally in the minor, the second part (trio) in the major key, to represent "the freedom of the disembodied spirit." Examples: Beethoven's Funeral March (Op. 26), Schubert's Funeral March (Op. 40, v.), Chopin's Funeral March. See also the movements "In modo d'una marcia" in Schumann's Quintet (Op. 44), Beethoven's Marcia Funèbre of the "Eroica" Symphony.

4. *The Triumphal or Festival March..*—The time is rather slower than that of the funeral march; its expression that of grandeur, pomp, and solemnity. The most celebrated examples are those of Beethoven's solemn march and chorus from the "Ruins of Athens," Cherubini's march from "Medea," Meyerbeer's coronation march from the "Prophète," and "Marche des Flambeaux," Gounod's marche solennelle from "La Reine de Saba," Wagner's "Tannhäuser," Huldigung's and Fridensmarsch, Lachner's march from "Catherina Comaro," and Suite in D minor.

5. *Religious Marches.*—These appear in operas and oratorios. (Compare Mozart's march in "Idomeneo," "Il Flauto Magico;" Beethoven's "Mount of Olives;" Mendelssohn's War-March of the Priests in "Athalia," etc.)

6. *National Marches.*—These are generally founded on national airs. Excellent examples are the Hungarian Rakoczy March, Schubert's Hungarian March (Op. 55), Beethoven's Turkish March (Op. 113), Weber's Gipsies' March from "Preciosa," etc.

SONGS WITHOUT WORDS.

These are piano-forte pieces of one movement, generally short, and appearing with regard to form and æsthetic intention to be an imitation of the song; consequently they have a lyrical expression, and the melody is accompanied in a refined and artistic manner. The name (in some respects a paradox, in as far as no song, properly speaking, can exist without words—the words being the reason of the existence of the song) was, according to private information given by a member of the family of Mendelssohn, who introduced these little compositions in this garb for the first time in 1831. The "Songs without words" soon obtained a universal recognition and approbation, and are now accepted as musical household words. With regard to their contents, Mendelssohn's "Songs without words" are not new, inasmuch as Beethoven's Bagatelles (see Op. 33, Nos. 4 and 6; Op. 119, No. 4; Op. 126, No. 3), and Field's Nocturnes contain similar matter, which, however, was not worked out in such detail or with such extreme care.

The "Songs without words" were imitated in numberless instances, but no composer after Mendelssohn succeeded in giving to them such absolute finish and roundness of form, combined with such pure, genuine sentiment. To only a few of Mendelssohn's "Songs without words" names were given by the composer himself.*

ETUDE (STUDY).

The Etude or Study, originally invented by Bach, has in course of time grown to great and even important proportions. At first it was intended solely for practice, for acquiring proficiency in certain passages. Clementi (1752-1832), in his "Gradus ad Parnassum," extended its sphere, and introduced fugues, toccatas, and canons. His pupil, John Baptist Cramer (1771-1858), greatly influenced by Mozart, sought to infuse what in reference to the students might be called a philanthropic spirit into the Study; for he introduced into it pleasant melody, harmony, and elegance, in which points Clementi was somewhat deficient. After Cramer's came the useful but somewhat dry technical Studies of Czerny, Herz, and Kalkbrenner. Moscheles (1794-1870) altered this form again, and greatly developed and enlarged Cramer's idea; till at last the beautiful and excellent Studies of Chopin, Henselt, Liszt, and Thalberg appear in a form which not only commands respect but excites popular admiration.

IDYLL, ETC.

The *Idyll, Eclogue,* and *Villanella* are short pastorals; the *Dithyramb* (W. Tomaschek, 1774-1850) and *Rhapsody* (Henselt, Brahms, Liszt) appear as an endeavor to portray by sounds the peculiar dactylic form of versification. *Impromptus* (Schubert, Taubert, Chopin), *Intermezzi*, and *Sketches* (Bennett, Schumann, Heller) are free forms, sometimes approaching the scherzo, at others again showing affinity with the smaller romantic pieces.

In poetry *Idyll* is a short pastoral poem, written in an elevated and highly finished style. *Eclogue* means in poetry a pastoral composition, in which shepherds are introduced conversing with each other; a bucolic. *Villanella* is a country (pastoral) tune. *Dithyrambus*, actually an ancient Greek hymn in honor of Bacchus, usually sung by a band of revellers to a flute accompaniment. *Rhapsody*, a disconnected series

---

* The general public ever anxious to know the composer's meaning, are at the same time not less desirous to have a *name* for each piece. All manner of fantastic, nonsensical names have been bestowed upon Mendelssohn's "Songs without words;" the names given by Stephen Heller to these popular gems are, however, an honorable exception to these worthless titles. They are as follows:—1. Sweet Remembrance; 2. Regret; 3. The Hunt; 4. Confidence; 5. Disquiet: 7. Contemplation; 8. Restlessness; 9. Consolation; 10. The Wanderer; 11. The Rivulet; 13. The Evening Star; 14. Lost Happiness; 15. The Harp of the Poet; 16. Hope; 17. Appassionata; 19. On the Shore; 20. The Vision; 21. Presto Agitato: 22. The Sorrowful Soul; 23. Triumphal Chant; 24. The Flight; 25. May Breezes; 26. The Departure; 27. Funeral March; 28. Morning Song; 30. Spring Song; 31. Meditation; 32. Lost Illusions; 33. The Pilgrim's Song; 34. The Spinning Song; 35. The Wail of the Shepherd; 36. Serenade; 37. A Reverie; 38. The Farewell; 39. Passion; 40. Elegy; 41. The Return; 42. Songs of the Traveller. (Nos. 6, 12, 18, 29 retain the names given by the author.) See also E. Pauer's "Harmonious Ideas;" "Poetical Mottoes for Mendelssohn's Songs without Words."

of sentences, a rambling composition. *Impromptu* (from the Latin *in promptu*, "in readiness"), a piece made off-hand at the moment or without any previous study, *Intermezzo* (see Vocal music). *Sketch* (Fr. *Esquiese;* Ger. *Skizze*), an outline or general delineation of anything.

POTPOURRI.

The Potpourri, Quodlibet, Melange, and Pasticcio, are pieces of uncertain length, put together in a loose, easy manner, and consisting of all possible popular airs. On the Continent such pieces are often performed by orchestras in public gardens, and a good deal of ingenuity has been shown in comic potpourris by Hamm, Küffner, and others. The potpourris and mélanges for piano-forte were introduced by Louis Emanuel Jadin in the beginning of this century. (Compare the well-known potpourri by Hamm, "Der lustige Figaro.")

DANCE MUSIC.

I.

OLD DANCES.

DANCE music, in its various branches, has influenced the musical art in a greater degree than is generally believed. Not only does the orchestra owe its existence to dance music, but the delightful rhythmical animation, which is one of the principal charms of modern music, is the result of the respective dance measures, such as minuets and others, adopted for the symphony, the sonata, etc.; the suite, for instance, is entirely a combination of dance movements. The dances are naturally to be divided into two classes, the *old* and the *modern* or *national*. Among the old dances are included all those which are now out of fashion and obsolete. In the case of some it is not easy even to describe them accurately. The first that require notice are the mediæval dances. France, Italy, and Spain had a great similarity in their dance music, Germany and England being rather behindhand in that branch of art; indeed the chief English dances, like the *Courante, Brawl, Pavan*, etc., were foreign importations.

ALLEMANDE.

The *Allemande* is, as its name implies, of German origin. There are two completely different kinds of allemandes: the first, one in two-four time, which is danced by the peasants of Swabia and Switzerland, and the second the allemande of the suite. The characteristics of the latter are earnestness of expression and a moderately quick movement. It ought to possess a rich harmony; and should in fact convey the feeling of "a certain contentment and quiet cheerfulness." The allemandes of Sebastian Bach are masterpieces, and have never been surpassed. The allemande follows the prelude, and always stands before the courante.

COURANTE (CORRENTE).

The *Courante* or *Corrente* is either of French or Italian origin. According to its name, which is derived from the French *courir*, or the Italian *correre*, its chief expression ought to give the idea of running. Mattheson, the well-known contemporary of Handel, describes it in the following quaint manner: "The passion or temper which is expressed in the courante is that of a sweet hope, and we detect in it something hardy, ambitious, yet cheerful. On the violin the courante is confined by no limits, but tries to do honor to its name by an incessant bustle and hurry, but yet in such a way that tenderness and grace are not absent. In France they preferred the courante played on the lute; but in Germany the masters set it for the clavecin. For dancing courantes the French invented the best tunes." Bach's and Handel's courantes are written either in three-two or three-four time; and it is usual to find doubles or variations added to them.

BOURRÉE.

According to the best authorities, the native land of this dance is Auvergne; but some writers designate as its home the Basque Provinces in Spain, where it is known by the name of Borea. Mattheson describes it as having "a cheerful and merry character; more fluent, smooth, sliding, and connected than the gavotte. The peculiarity of the bourrée is a certain jovial and pleasant expression, coupled with an air of happy carelessness—an easy though not vulgar movement." The bourrée is in two-four or common time, and is adapted to the dactylic metre, where two short notes follow a long one. In England the bourrée is represented by the popular hornpipe.

GAVOTTE.

The *Gavot* or *Gavotte* has a great similarity with the Bourrée. The actual difference between a bourrée and a gavotte is that the former begins on the last or unaccented part of the bar, while the latter begins with the heavy or accented part of the second half. The gavotte is of French origin; it is the dance of the Gavots or *Gap-men*, the inhabitants of the town of Gap, in the Haute-Alpes. It was mostly used for theatrical purposes, seldom as a social dance. Mattheson tells us "the expression should be that of a right jubilant joy; the 'jumping' and by no means the 'running' movement is a particular feature of it." The gavottes of Sebastian Bach are very excellent models, and have attained universal popularity. Bach and other composers add to several of their gavottes a musetta or bagpipe-tune. The peculiarity of the *Musetta* is that the fundamental bass never changes; and thus the piece imitates the quaint monotonous effect of the bagpipe.

CEBELL.

"The name of an air or theme in common time of four-bar phrases, forming a subject upon which to execute 'divisions' upon the lute or violin. This style of air, although frequently found in books for the violin in the seventeenth century, is now obsolete; its principal feature was the alternation of grave and acute notes which formed the several strains."*

SARABANDE.

The *Sarabande* is of Spanish origin; and was transferred to Italy, where it altered its primary expression in being converted into a stately, earnest and solemn dance, very different from its characteristic expression in Spain. When we read that the Spanish sarabande was danced with castanets, we can scarcely reconcile such an accompaniment with the *grandezza*, the quiet grandeur, which predominates in Handel's and Bach's sarabandes. The sarabande may be called the "central body" of the suite, as it is the one slow movement round which the quicker movements—the prelude, allemande, and courante on the one side, and the gavotte and gigue on the other—revolve. Shakespeare speaks of it in "Much Ado About Nothing" as "a measure full of state and ancientry;" and indeed it can hardly be more happily described. Sebastian Bach treated the sarabande as the principal and most important piece of the suite, and bestowed on it an amount of care that was extraordinary even for that ever-conscientious composer; working it out in the most minute detail. Indeed the sarabandes of the Second, Third, and Sixth English Suites are models of refined workmanship and exquisite taste. Handel's celebrated air "Lascia che piango" was a sarabande from his opera "Almira," and appeared again six years later as Almirena's air in the opera "Rinaldo."

GIGUE.

This lively dance is also written zigg, jig, giga, gigue, gicque, schick, quique: but gigue is now the universally adopted way of writing the name. Nägeli in his Lectures, p. 115, says: "The suite with all its dance tunes required also an artistically worked piece of more solid construction, something like the fugue. As all the preceding dance movements of the suite, such as allemande, courante, sarabande, gavotte, bourrée, had been divided into two parts of equal length, it was considered desirable that the gigue should also be divided in the same manner, and that the first part ought to close on the dominant; otherwise, almost all the devices followed out in the fugue were also applied to the gigue, and thus a favorable result was gained: a lively piece with a solid construction, resembling a dance movement, yet possessing also a deeper interest for the connoisseur." There are four different kinds of gigues: (1) the English; (2) the Spanish, also called Loures; (3) the Canaries; and (4) the Italian giga. According to another authority the "jig" was formerly the dance tune used during the performance of the rope-dancers. At present the name of jig is given to any dance music of a lively, droll, and grotesque expression. The Spanish gigues or loures are slower, and have a "somewhat pompous and magniloquent expression, a vain and inflated tune," as Mattheson quaintly calls it. The Canaries are full of life and bustle, but ought to have somewhat of a simple, even childish expression. The Italian giga is that used by Handel, and sometimes also by Bach. This form has retained a certain influence on modern music. (See the last movement of Beethoven's "Kreutzer" Sonata.)

---

* See Stainer and Barrett's "Dictionary of Musical Terms," p. 81.

ANGLOISE.

The name Angloise was formerly given to three kinds of English dances: (a) the Country dance; (b) to the Ballad, and (c) to the Hornpipe. Mattheson, in his "Kern melodischer Wissenschaft," p. 117, says: "The principal quality of the Angloise is 'obstinacy,' but this quality is accompanied by an expression of generosity and good-nature." The *Country dance* is the dance of the peasants, for which all possible national and dramatic airs are used. The Ballad is a song, to the tune of which people danced, as in France (Chansons de danse). The Hornpipe is the sailor's dance (see Hornpipe and Bourrée).

BRAWL.

The Brawl is an antiquated French dance (Branle), in which the whole company joined—not unlike the modern cotillon. The old writers described it as being not so lively as the courantes or galliards, but danced merely by bending the knees, not by jumping with the feet. Towards the end of the sixteenth century it was customary to dance during the evening several kinds of Branles: the Branle double (also called Branle common), the Branle simple, the Branlegai, and finally the Branle de Bourgogne, or Branle de Champagne. The old people danced the Branle double, the young married couples the Branle de Bourgogne. Thoinet Arbeau mentions in his "Orchésographie" (Langres, 1588) the following kinds of Branles: (1) Branle double; (2) Branle simple; (3) Branle gai (in triple time); (4) Branle de haut Barrois; (5) Branle coupé, also called "Cassandra," "Pinagay," "Charlotte," "Branle de la Guerre," "Aridan;" (6) Branle de Poitou (in triple time); (7) Branle écossais; (8) Branle, called "Triori;" (9) Branle de Matta; (10) Branle des Blanchisseuses (the Washerwomen's Branle); (11) Branle Margueritotte; (12) Branle des Hermites; (13) Branle des Flambeaux; (14) Branle des Sabots; (15) Branle des Chevaux; (16) Branle de la Moutarde; (17) Branle de la Haie; (18) Branle de l'Official.

CHACONNE.

The origin of the Chaconne or Ciaccona is variously stated. It is not quite certain whether it derives its origin from Italy or Spain. The name itself is described as coming from the Italian *cieco*, which means "blind;" and it is said that the inventor of the ciaccona was blind. It is also asserted that *chaconne* comes from the Arabic, and means "the dance of the king." According to Mattheson ("Vollkommener Capellmeister," p. 233), "the dance 'Chaconne' takes its name from the Spanish Admiral Chacon, commanding the fleet, 1721, in America." Again, Littré says that the name comes from the Basque *chocuna*, "pretty." The music of the chaconne is in three-four time. It has a very sedate movement, and has the peculiarity that an air of four, sometimes eight bars, with an agreeable melody and particularly well-marked rhythm, is performed in the bass; this air is, like in the ground, incessantly repeated, while the upper part is varied, the variations being called couplets. Sometimes a certain relief is brought into it by the interpolation of a short phrase; but this is rarely applied. The most celebrated chaconnes are those of Bach, Couperin, and Handel. In England it was called "the chacon," and was danced like the sarabande or measure, of which Queen Elizabeth was very fond.

MINUET.

In France this dance is called "le menuet;" in Italy, "minuetto." It is said to have come originally from the French province of Poitou. The name itself is derived from the Latin *minutus*, "small," and this name was given on account of the short steps peculiar to it. The minuet is distinguished for its graceful, noble, and dignified expression—it was especially the dance of the nobility, and every ball was opened with it; its prevailing character was a moderate cheerfulness. To give variety to the minuet, a second part was generally composed for it, which offered a certain contrast to the first. This second part is called "trio," because, while formerly the minuet was written for two parts only—mostly for a violin and a bass—the second division was set for three parts. We sometimes, but rarely, meet with the minuet in the suite; but it had been unconditionally accepted in the other cyclical forms, such as the sonata, symphony, serenade, cassazione, etc. Haydn, Mozart, and Beethoven made splendid use of the minuet. In Haydn's hand the minuet received another character; whereas before his time it had a somewhat aristocratic expression, Haydn, without lowering or vulgarizing it, imparted to it a popular tone, a simple and jovial manner. With him it has essentially a cheerful and good-natured expression. Mozart understood how to imbue it with a more refined wit and an artistic character; and Beethoven managed to give an indescribable charm to his minuets. Although in his later works the scherzo took the place of the minuet, he uses it again in his Eighth Symphony. The minuet must therefore be recognized as one of the principal and most important dances among those which in a great degree influenced instrumental music.

PASSACAGLIO.

The Passacaglio was called in French "passecaille." According to some old writers the name is also pronounced "passagallo," which means in German, "Hahnentrapp," or the trotting of the cock. This last term was probably an illusion to the mode in which the passacaglio was danced. The passecaille has a certain resemblance to the chaconne, in so far as the bass ought to contain the melody, and the upper part furnish variations to it, which, like those in the chaconne, are called couplets. The old writers, Mattheson, Walther, and Koch, differ in their opinion as to the quicker or slower time of the passacaglio.

PASSAMEZZO.

The Passamezzo is an old Italian dance, with a soft and quiet expression. Prætorius and Walther give valuable information concerning it. The former says: "*Passamezzo a possando, transcendo*, meaning that he who dances it ought to proceed quietly and gradually; and just as a galliard has five steps, and is therefore called 'cinquepas' (cinquepace), so also has the passamezzo not half this number, 'quasi dicas,' 'mezzo passa,' as if you called it 'half-step.'" Walther adds; "*Passamezzo*, an old Italian dance, in which the dancer went quietly through the room; also an old Italian song, to which people danced." The passamezzo is now completely forgotten.

PASSEPIED.

The Passepied was formerly the dance of the Breton sailors. The expression of the passepied is that of merriment and liveliness, or as Mattheson expresses it, "The character of the passepied indicates an approach to negligence; it ought to show a certain vacillation and unsteadiness, not passion or excitement; but such negligence must be expressive not of ill-humor and caprice, but of good-nature and joviality." The passepied is in three-eight or three-four time, and generally alternates with a second passepied of the same length; if the first is in the minor key the second is set in the major key, and *vice versâ*. When the passepied is introduced in a suite, it takes the place of the gavotte or bourrée; that is, it comes between the sarabande and the gigue.

According to some writers, passepied (English "paspy"—compare the example of Purcell and Croft, given in the "Dictionary of Musical Terms," by J. Stainer and W. A. Barrett, p. 343) is identical with passamezzo, although "to proceed quietly and gradually" and again "merriment and liveliness" do not actually harmonize.

PAVAN.

The Pavana, *pava d'Espagne*, pavin or pavan, is an extraordinary dance. According to the Old English Encyclopædia, "the pavan is a grave dance, common among the Spaniards." In this dance the performers described a kind of wheel before each other; the gentlemen danced it with cap and sword, princes in their state robes, and the ladies with long trains, the movements resembling the stately step of the peacock, in Italian called "pavone." The *Paduaná* is a similar grave and stately dance, which, however, may take its name from Padua, in Italy.

GALLIARD.

The name Galliard is derived, according to some old writers, from *valiarda* (Lat. *validus*), "strong." In the Italian and French languages *gagliarda* or *gaillard* means, "merry, jolly, free, cheerful, fresh, and healthy;" and such in fact ought to be the expression of this dance. Some musical historians say that Rome was the birthplace of the galliard, and that the name of *Romanesca* was then given to it; but this may be doubted, because the tune which we know under the name Romanesca is not merry or cheerful, but rather the reverse. The gaillarde par terre was also called *Tourdion*.

RIGAUDON.

The Rigaudon, called in English "Rigadoon," is an old French dance, to which it was the custom to sing an accompaniment. The rigaudon is written in common time, and had its origin in Provence. The character of the rigaudon is merry and cheerful; the quickest notes are quavers. According to Th. Lejarte, the rigaudon was named after its inventor, the dancing-master Monsieur Rigaud.

SICILIANO.

A kind of melody to which the Sicilian peasants were accustomed to dance. Its character is that of rural simplicity and tenderness. It is set in six-eight time; but its movement is rather slower than that of the pastorale. The rhythm of the Siciliano was also used for vocal pieces; thus we find beautiful examples in Handel's "Susanna" and "Theodora."

A cursory glance at the old dances is sufficient to convince us that they were of the greatest possible importance to the progress of instrumental music. Not only did the separate character each of them possessed lend a peculiar charm to their introduction and adaptation for the cyclical forms, but the composer learned by their means to invent better and more fascinating tunes. Under the garb of a passacaglio or a chaconne, it was pleasant to hear and admire contrapuntal feats, whilst on the other hand the minuet offered to Haydn, Mozart, and Beethoven a welcome opportunity to suffuse their works with an agreeable good-nature. The old dance movements brought life, grace, and rhythmical beauty into instrumental music; and thus we perceive that the music of the people becomes a most important agent in enhancing the charm of instrumental music generally, in widening its sphere by the simplest and most welcome means, and in consolidating its popularity.

THE OLD DANCE MOVEMENTS.

Classified with respect to their time and rhythmical expression.

DANCE MUSIC. 153

II.
MODERN AND NATIONAL DANCES.

GERMAN DANCES.

ALTHOUGH the Germans are certainly one of the most musical nations, they cannot boast of such a variety of dances as other nations (the Spaniards, for instance) possess. The chief dance of the Germans is "*der Walzer.*" This again we find in different forms in Germany proper, Styria and Tyrol. The name Walzer comes from the German *wälzen*, " to revolve," or more literally, " to roll." The German, Styrian, and Tyrolese valses are all slow and expressive of a quiet and moderate enjoyment. The Styrian and Tyrolese valses sometimes change the slow movement into a quicker one. The music here is expressive of the dancing movement, in so far as the slower part accompanies the more graceful turns of the dancing pair. The real German Walzer (introduced 1787), however, does not introduce such changes of movement or figures, but goes on placidly and somewhat pedantically. The *Styrian* Walzer of Lanner (Op. 6, 11, 165, 202) are models of a true characteristic expression; and the rustic valses of Beethoven, the so-called "*Deutsche*" or "*Ländler*" by Mozart, Beethoven, Schubert, and the Six Valses by C. M. von Weber, convey the most accurate idea of what a real German valse should be.

A most interesting valse (from the Upper Palatinate, Bavaria) is called " Zweifacher " und " Grad und Ungrad:"—

(Compare L. Köhler, "Die Tänze aller Nationen.") The modern *Valse*, now generally called "Vienna" or "Quick Valse," is quite different from the above-mentioned kind. The old valse appears more like an animated minuet, whilst the modern valse possesses fire, energy, and a certain tender expression. Weber has removed the monotony and *Philistinism* from the former dance. In his beautiful "Invitation à la Valse" we find the root of all the valses which Lanner, Strauss, Labitzky, Gungl and others wrote. A most unnatural valse, a kind of anomaly, is the "Valse à deux temps." It is a vain attempt to amalgamate the rhythm of the galop with that of the valse; but whilst the valse in three-four time is expressive of a graceful circular movement, the specialty of the *Galop* is that of alternating movement in a line with *sharp* and *angular* turns. The only result of its introduction was to accelerate the movement of the valse in an exaggerated degree and to rob it of all its natural grace.

ENGLISH DANCES.

The dances common in England in old days, such as the *Brawl*, the *Measure*, the *Cushion-dance*, the *Maypole*, or *Morris-dance*, the *Pavan*, the *Galliard*, were all foreign importations; the only real English dances are, the *Country-dance*, the *Hornpipe*, and the *Reel*, which latter belongs also to the Scotch and Irish—to the former nation especially. The country-dance consisted of different movements, and is a kind of suite. Most probably it was formerly danced at once by the whole company, and its charm may have been enhanced by pantomimic figures and fancy costumes. The *Country-dance* is said to have been adopted by the French under the name of *contredanse*. Some writers, however, assert that the name *contredanse* illustrates the manner in which the performers danced opposite each other without taking hands. The country-dance has to some extent gone out of fashion, though in the rural districts it is not yet obsolete. The *Hornpipe* was originally a Scotch dance, and takes its name from the horn or bagpipe on which the tune is played. The name "hornpipe" is now generally given to sailors' dances which are written in the common time, and through their quaint and cheery rhythm possess a peculiar charm. The *Reel* is a dance which is to be found in England, but which belongs more particularly to Scotland, though also met with in Ireland, Sweden, Norway, and Denmark. The word itself is Saxon, *reol*, and means, like the verb *reel* in English, "to stagger." The number of Scotch reels is quite enormous; every clan, nay, almost every great Scottish family, possesses its particular reel, as it has its coat-of-arms. The monotony, harshness, and barbarous bass of the reel make it anything but pleasing. There is a sort of rough and savage character in it; but as the exponent of a national expression it demands attention.

ENGLISH DANCE (1577).

COUNTRY-DANCE TUNE (about 1300).

NORWEGIAN AND SWEDISH DANCES.

Different collections of Scandinavian dance-tunes show that the Norwegians possess three kinds of dances: first, the *Spring-dance*, or *Hopping-dance*, in three-four time; secondly, the so-called *Dance-tunes* in two-four time; and thirdly, the *Reels*. In all these there is an eminent brightness and precision of rhythmical expression. The spring-dances are written either for a clarinet and bass instrument, or perhaps for a bagpipe. The dance-tunes are sung by the dancers themselves, and are rather slower. The reel is here, as in Sweden, generally danced by the sailors. Everything that has been said about Norway applies also to Sweden and Denmark. The dance melodies are, however, more in use in Sweden, and the melodies of the Dalecarlians—strictly, Dalarnes, which means literally *Dale-carles*, "inhabitants of the dale or valley"—enjoy a great celebrity. The Swedish dance melodies express more of a pastoral character than those of the Norwegians and Danes.

WALLACHIAN, MOLDAVIAN, AND ROUMANIAN DANCES.

All these are written in two-four time, and have a distinct character from all other national dances. Generally, voices singing the tune accompany the dance. Each profession has its own dance-tune;

thus we find a shepherd's, a soldier's, and a lover's dance. The last-mentioned is known by the generic name of *Sentimental dance*. We find in the character of the northern dances a suggestion of that popular instrument the bagpipe. In the south we meet with the violin, the clarinet, the violoncello, sometimes the flute, and most particularly the so-called Hackbrett, the dulcimer, or German psalterium. This venerable instrument dates from the eleventh century, and is now almost confined to the gipsies, or Hungarian bands. The character of the Roumanian, Wallachian, and Moldavian dance music is expressive of a tender feeling, a cheerfulness not untinged with a certain melancholy, and in some parts with a martial expression.

ITALIAN DANCES.

Italy, though it has been called the cradle of music, does not possess many national dances. Strictly speaking, there are only *two* dances which are genuinely Italian, the *Tarantella* and the *Monferina*. The *Saltarello*, which is danced in Rome, is a Spanish importation; and the *Bergamasca* is merely known to the inhabitants of the district of Bergamo, and can therefore not be called a national, but merely a provincial dance. The instruments used for playing the tunes are the guitar or mandolina, the tambourine, and the castanets. Of the tarantella we find a description in Goethe's "Italian Journey." He says, "The tarantella is a great favorite of the girls belonging to the middle and lower classes of Naples. Three persons are required to dance it: one beats the tambourine and shakes its bells from time to time in the intervals of striking the parchment; the two others, with castanets in their hands, dance the simple steps. The tarantella, like almost all popular dances, does not consist of regular steps; the girls rather walk or move rhythmically, turning round, changing places, or tripping about, whilst they keep opposite each other. The tarantella is merely an amusement for girls—no boy would touch a tambourine or dance to it; the girls, however, pass their pleasantest hours in dancing the tarantella, and it has often served as a distraction for melancholy. It is also considered an excellent remedy for the bite of a peculiar spider. This insect's bite heals only through the effects of exercise, which this dance liberally furnishes; but again, the passion for the dance itself is known to have grown into a sort of mania. It is a general opinion that the tarantella is called after the above-named spider, the tarantula; but this opinion is false—both spider and dance came from the province Tarento, and both have been named after their native region. There is no real connection between the name of the provincial spider and the provincial dance." From the best examples of tarantella tunes we perceive that singing and dancing proceed together; and no more beautiful and genial tarantella of its kind could be named than the delightful tarantella of Rossini ("Soirées musicales"). The monferina is a cheerful and lively dance-tune in six-eight time. The saltarella was originally a Spanish dance. The name is derived from *saltare*, which means "to jump." The character of the saltarella is very much like that of the tarantella. Its peculiar rhythm and fiery animation are very tempting to composers; and we detect its influence in the last movement of Mendelssohn's so-called Italian Symphony. A certain analogy exists between the gigue and the saltarella.

The monferina, belonging to the ancient Duchy of Montferrat, and highly popular in the town of Monferrato (see Twelve Monferrines by M. Clementi, Op. 49), is a cheerful dance of simple expression in six-eight time:—

MONFERRINE (No. 5). CLEMENTI. *Allegretto.*

SPANISH DANCES.

Spanish dances are to be reckoned among the most beautiful and original. The Spaniards possess all the different qualities essentially necessary for excellence in dancing, especially natural grace with a certain composure and dignity of deportment; besides, the somewhat indolent habits of the nation are rather more favorable to dancing and amusement than to close and continued application to business and work. The chief Spanish dances are the *Seguidillas* (sequences), the *Fandango*, and the *Bolero*.

The *Seguidillas* might be considered as the original and model of all the present Spanish national dances, and its description applies, with but slight modifications only, to the not less-known fandango and bolero.

The manner of dancing the seguidillas is the following: During the prelude of the guitar, the dancers, mostly clad in the picturesque costume of the *majo* and the *maja*, take their places, standing opposite each other in two rows, and not farther than three or four steps; the first verse of the *copla* is sung whilst the dancers are standing still; the voice stops, the guitar now takes up the real dance-tune, and with its fourth bar the singers join with the song of the seguidillas, accompanied by the indispensable sound of the castanets. The general effect is heightened by the elegant swinging and elastic step of the dance, the graceful moving forward and backward, movements indicating the tender playfulness and affectionate animation of loving couples. The steps themselves consist of a peculiar mixture of the movements of the fandango, the jota, and the noisy taconeos. The first part of the seguidillas finishes with the ninth bar; then follows a short pause, filled up by soft chords on the guitar. Part the second begins with the dancers changing places without touching hands. With a few slight variations the figures of the first part are now repeated; and with the ninth bar of the third and last part the music and the dance both stop abruptly; and it is one of the principal rules of this dance that with the last note the performers rest immovably in their position. The seguidillas obtained a general popularity in the Spanish kingdom.

The *Fandango* is on the whole more or less a modification of the seguidillas, and it requires a very experienced eye to find out the few instances in which a real difference shows itself. The movement of the fandango is slow, and in six-eight time. It is danced by two persons clapping the castanets.

The construction of the *Bolero* is very similar to that of the seguidillas, the only difference being a slower, more minuet-like step. It was invented in 1780 by Don Sebastian Zerezo, one of the most famous Spanish dancers. The bolero is a more dignified and quiet dance than the fandango, and is performed only by two persons. Its name is derived from the Spanish verb *volero*, "to fly," and was most probably given on account of some of its light, almost flying movements.

La Madrilena, "dance of Madrid," *la Cachuca, Gitana, Jota Aragoneza*, are dances which were introduced into ballets for demonstrating the particular artistic excellence of the famous dancers Mlles. Cerrito, Ellsler, Taglioni, and others.

FRENCH DANCES.

Of all the European nations, France bestowed the greatest care and attention on the dance, considering it as a separate and important branch of art, and recognizing with liberal honors and rewards the merits of various great dancing-masters. Among the most popular of modern French dances comes first of all the *Contredanse*. The French contredanse was introduced into France in 1710 by an English dancing-master. The different melodies of the contredanse had each a special name; but as there were a great many of these tunes the most favorite ones were ultimately selected, and these were then united to form the *Quadrille*. For this reason we may compare the quadrille with a sonata of five or six movements. Each of these figures, called *le pantalon, la poule, l'été, la trénise* or *la pastourelle*, and *le finale*, has a special characteristic expression. Pantalon comes from a little verse which was sung to a favorite tune of a contredanse. This melody became so popular that it was introduced in every quadrille, and the figure was called shortly "pantalon." The name "été" is an abridgment of a celebrated contredanse, "Le pas d'été," introduced in 1800. In 1802, Jullien, a French dancing-master, introduced a contredanse in the second part of which the company supplemented the tune with the imitation of the cackling of a hen. This jest became popular, and its memory was perpetuated in the name "poule." Later, the vocal accompaniment was discontinued; but the movements of the figure were retained, and with them its name. The figure "la trénise" was invented in 1800 by Trenitz, an excellent Berlin dancing-master. The name "pastourelle" was given to the tune in six-eight time for its similarity to pastoral music, or the "villanelle."

During the first decade of this century the contredanses partly disappeared from the ballrooms, and their place was filled by the lively *Ecossaises*. The écossaise is a much older dance than the contredanse. We perceive this from the letters of Voltaire, who praises his niece, Mlle. Denis, for her skillful and elegant dancing of the écossaise. Originally the écossaise came from Scotland, and was introduced by French dancing-masters into different ballets, and afterwards adopted for the ball-room. The difference between the specific French dances and those of other nations is particularly that the Frenchman prefers dancing opposite to his partner, a manner highly favorable for the display of lively gesticulation and pantomimic action. Between 1820 and 1840 the German round dances, such as the *Valse*, the *Galop*, the Polish *Mazurek, Polonaise*, and the Bohemian *Polka*, rivaled the French *Minuet* and *Contredanse*, and were readily accepted by the majority of Frenchmen. The greatest point of perfection the French dances reached was in the time of Louis XIV. The *Schottisch* is a senseless mixture of a polka and a slow valse. *Les Lanciers* is an adaptation of the French quadrille called the lancers; *la Redowa* is the Bohemian redowak; *la Polka* is the Bohemian polka, called *Trasák* (la Polka tremblante).

BOHEMIAN DANCES.

Two Bohemian dances belong to a famous political period—namely, to that of the war of the Hussites. However, only the names of these two dances are still known, and live in the hearts of the people; the figures and general execution of the dances have been completely forgotten. One of these dances is called the *Chodowska*, and is full of a warlike expression—at least, so far as can be judged from the style of its music. The name is derived from the peasants living near to the Bohemian forest, the Chodowe. The other of these two ancient political dances is the *Husitska*, "dance of the Hussites." It belonged exclusively to that sect. Another peculiar and strange custom of the Bohemians was to sing sacred songs during the dance. The *Skákavá*, or jump-dance, was generally accompanied by a religious song, distinguished by a simple touching melody, later adopted by the Hungarians. The *Sousedska*, very similar to the Austrian *Ländler*, a rustic dance, was peculiar for the dancers scarcely moving from the place they took on beginning. The sousedska was not only exceedingly graceful in point of the movements, but also for its highly ingratiating and pleasing music.

The world-wide renowned *Polka* dates from a very recent time. It was about 1830 that Anna Slezak, an upper servant of a rich farmer at Elbeteinitz, near Prague, invented this dance. The room in which she tried her new invention being very small, the movements of her feet were necessarily short, and thus the dance received the name *pulka*, anglicé " half." As the pulka met with an enthusiastic reception in Paris, it is most likely that the French, ever ready to accommodate any foreign name to their own language, changed *pulka* into *polka*. The manner in which the polka is danced in Bohemia is, however, very different from that accepted in other countries. The Bohemians dance the polka with retardation and acceleration of the step, and try to keep strict time with the music, which has to be performed in a free, *tempo rubato* style.

The *Umrlec* (Todtentanz) was, up to the last decades of the eighteenth century, danced by night in the cemeteries.

The *Rejdowák* (Radowa, Radowaczka) is identical with the old German dance Ridewauz, French Rotuenge.

The *Baborak* or Baboraka was introduced from Bavaria, the Stajrys from Styria.

RUSSIAN DANCES.

In Russia almost every district claims a special dance of its own. These dances, however, contain nothing very original. The best-known Russian dances are the *Golubez*, " dove-dance," the *Russjaka*, and the *Cossack*. The last-mentioned is performed by two persons only, who approach each other and retire in turn, accompanying the figures with a very lively pantomime. The dance-tune, generally in two-four time and in the minor key, excels in most striking contrasts.

POLISH DANCES.

The principal Polish dances are the *Polonaise* and the *Mazurek* (mazure, mazurka). Owing to their agreeable and striking rhythmical expression, they have been adapted by almost every composer. The polonaise expresses the national spirit and character—chivalry, grandeur, and stateliness; the cadence with which each part closes indicates the deep bow of the gentleman, and the graceful courtesy of the lady. The polonaise is the court-dance *par excellence;* the *Marche aux flambeaux* and the *Danses de cérémonie* are indeed nothing more than polonaises; and their gravity and pomp, with the total absence of any lively movement, are characteristic of court etiquette and the reserved and official manner considered necessary at court festivals. The name Mazurka is derived from Masureks, the inhabitants of the district of Massovia. The mazurka (¾ or ⅜ time) has been ennobled, nay, almost idealized, in its music by Chopin. The clinking together of the spurs, a feature in this dance, comes always on the second crotchet. It is the rhythmical expression that lends its great charm to this national dance. The *Cracoviac* (¾ time) belongs to the district of Cracow.

HUNGARIAN DANCES.

The dances of the Hungarians are of quite a special kind, and show a certain similarity to those of the Cossacks. The most remarkable dance of the Hungarians is undoubtedly the *Csárdás;* it begins with a slow movement (Lassù) and becomes by degrees livelier and wilder (Fris), but has throughout a certain chivalrous and ceremonious air. We possess a very great number of Hungarian dance-tunes; generally they are highly original, but we sometimes meet with a distant echo of Spanish music; which may result from the fact that the Hungarian musicians belong chiefly to the race of gipsies, many of whom are to be found in Spain.

CONCLUDING REMARKS.

With respect to the different character of various kinds of dance music we shall find that each expresses, like all the other arts, the spirit of the time in which it originated and was used. We find the sarabandes, the minuets, the gavottes, musettes, and all the other old dance movements in fashion at the beginning of the eighteenth century characteristic of a measured dignity, of a certain gravity, and of that most peculiar quaint humor which were the typical expression of the period. In the beginning of the present century we meet with an almost childlike simplicity, a certain sentimentality, which, however, was leavened by an admixture of cheerfulness. The dance-tunes of this time are meagre, pale and colorless, and devoid of striking characteristic expression. Weber at length struck a new, and indeed the right chord, in his splendid "Invitation à la Valse;" for in Weber's beautiful valse we recognize the natural expression of affection, whilst the previous dances were expressive of stiff etiquette, conventional manners, or of simplicity and quietness. Another feature, and a most interesting one, is that the modern dance as initiated by Weber expresses a certain melancholy feeling—and this increases its popularity.

Dance music brought life, animation, and its own charm into instrumental music. As *melody* is the chief attribute of vocal music, and as *harmony* is the chief ingredient, the soul of instrumental music, so the pervading principle of dance music is *rhythm;* and it is evident that each of these three different branches of musical art gains by adopting the special qualities of the others. The effect of vocal music is increased by the adaptation of rich harmony. Instrumental music will gain in expression and life by the cultivation of melody and rhythm; and dance music cannot but be ennobled by adorning itself with the attributes of melody and harmony. Vocal music is the exponent of our direct feeling; instrumental music appeals more immediately to our intellect; and dance music especially is associated with cheerfulness and joy.

LITERATURE.—Arbeau (Thoinot, pseudonym for Tehan Tabourot), "Orchésographie, Traité en forme de dialogue, par lequel toutes personnes peuvent facilement apprendre et pratiquer l'honnête exercice des dances;" Langres, 1588–1596; German translation by A. Czerwinski, Danzig, 1778. Bonin, "Neueste Art der galanten und theatralischen Tanzkunst," 1712. Meletaon, "Von der Nutzbarkeit des Tanzens;" Frankfurt and Leipzig, 1713. "The Dancing-Master, or Directions for Dancing Country-Dances, with the Tunes to each Dance, for the Treble Violin," sixteenth edition; London, 1716. Taubert, "Der rechtschaffene Tanzmeister;" Leipzig, 1717. Noverre (Jean-Georges), "Lettres sur la danse et les ballets; Lyon, 1760; Vienne, 1767; Paris, 1783; Copenhagen, 1803; Paris, 1807. Platter (Thomas und Felix), "Ein Beitrag zur Sittengeschichte des 18ten Jahrhunderts;" Basel, 1840. Waldau (Alfred), "Böhmische National Tänze;" Prag, 1860. Czerwinski (Albert), "Geschichte der Tanzkunst;" Leipzig, 1862.

APPENDIX.

MELODRAMA, MONODRAMA, DUODRAMA,

A MELODRAMA may in a general sense be defined as any play that is combined with music; in the stricter sense it is a kind of drama in which the dialogue is accompanied by instrumental music. The intention of the music is to heighten and intensify the impression produced by the spoken words, and also to give expression to those higher and deeper sentiments for which the word alone is insufficient. The music of the melodrama has no independent or strict forms. It is entirely subordinate to the declamation. It may continue after the words have ceased. It generally consists of very short phrases, sometimes even of only one or two sustained chords. Its great object is to portray in musical notes all that the orator expresses in words. If this recitation takes the form of a monologue the form of the melodrama is called *monodrama;* if two persons recite so as to form a dialogue, it receives the name of *duodrama.* The invention of the melodrama is generally attributed to Jean-Jacques Rousseau, whose melodrama "Pygmalion" (written about 1770) created such a sensation that the well-known German actor Brandes commissioned the poet Gerstenberg to write "Ariadne auf Naxos," which piece the composer Georg Benda (1721–1795) set to music. This melodrama met with such success that the poet Gotter wrote the melodrama "Medea," to which Benda also supplied the music. In quick succession followed the melodramas "Sophonisba," by Meissner, with music by Neefe; "Lampedo," by Lichtenberg, with music by the Abbé Vogler. Musical accompaniments have been written by B. A. Weber for Schiller's poem "Der Gang nach dem Eisenhammer," by Lindpaintner for Schiller's "Lied von der Glocke," and by Zumsteeg for Klopstock's "Frühling." The most noteworthy melodramatic applications of music as an accompaniment to speech are the two monologues in Mozart's opera "Zaide," Weber's Incantation Scene in "Der Freischütz," the same composer's opera "Preciosa," a scene in Beethoven's "Fidelio," Schumann's setting of Byron's "Manfred," and parts of Shakespeare's "Midsummer Night's Dream" set to music by Mendelssohn. Robert Schumann wrote music for two poems, of which the ballad "Der Haideknabe" is almost terrible in the tragic intensity of its effect. In one respect melodramatic treatment might be utilized for educational purposes in so far as pupils would gain freedom in elocution, whilst the musical student would learn the art of accompanying in a satisfactory manner. This union of speech and music is decidedly of great power, and offers a useful and agreeable amusement for young people.

CHAMBER-MUSIC.

According to our modern notions, chamber-music is defined as music for one or more instruments. Originally chamber-music was understood to be the music performed at royal courts and in the palaces of the nobles of the land, in *rooms* to which no one had access without special permission. The term was, however, also understood to designate a private musical performance at a court, to which privileged persons were invited. At first these performances were only executed by solo instrumentalists. Mattheson (1681–1764) says in his "Patriot," p. 64, "A stately harmony (music) may very well be executed by eight persons, namely, four vocalists, two violinists, one organist and one director (conductor); if the director can sing or play a part, seven persons will be enough. So many parts as the composer had set for the piece, so many performers were required." These older performances of chamber-music were confined (as they still are in our time) to secular works, and for this reason the style of the chamber-music differed alike from the sacred and from the dramatic style. In former time chamber-music included also vocal works, such as madrigals, cantate di camera, duetti di camera, indeed everything that did not belong to the church or the theatre. At present we apply the term chamber-music to instrumental pieces, such as sonatas for one or two instruments, trios, quartets, quintets, sestuors, septuors, etc., suites for the piano or violin, fantasias, toccatas, songs without words, indeed everything that belongs to the domain of solo performance; and we exclude from this category the concerto, overture, and symphony, whilst in earlier times these forms, as well as the concerto grosso, the cassazione, divertimento, serenade, notturno (see these forms) belonged to the class of chamber-music.

Three styles of music were always recognized: (1) the Sacred style or church music, (2) the Dramatic style or operatic music, and (3) the style of Chamber-music. Out of chamber-music has now grown a fourth style, namely, concert-music. The limited dimensions of the rooms in which chamber-music was performed also necessitated a peculiar style. Whilst the oratorio was adapted to the church or large halls, and the opera to the opera-house, chamber-music was originally intended for the private house, for the more limited family circle. The oratorio, like the opera, depends on the full orchestra and the chorus; its structure is planned on a larger, broader scale, whilst the chief interest of the chamber-music is found in the refined and artistic working out of the details on a regular systematic philosophical development of the principal subject. The oratorio depends on the enthusiasm of worship or a kind of devotional attention, whilst the dramatic style is founded on subjects which arouse our psychological interest: the chamber-music appeals more directly to our intellectuality (see Quartet and Thematic work). The chamber-music follows up its work through the smallest, most delicate details. The formal beauty reveals itself there in the happiest light; indeed, it is rather a work of intellectuality and refinement of taste, than of spontaneous inspiration or enthusiasm; it appeals more to the intellect than to the senses. Chamber-music, as shown in its best examples, by Haydn, Mozart, Beethoven, Mendelssohn, Schumann, and others, might well be called the philosophic phase of music.

DRAWING-ROOM MUSIC.

There can be not the slightest doubt that this particular style has a legitimate and even an important part to fulfil, and that it not only presents a great charm, but constitutes a musical necessity. Music, as an art, would never have reached the high degree of universal popularity it has obtained, had it been confined to symphonies, oratorios, and masses alone. The popular element of an art is always a very excellent agency to make the art universally beloved; and it is decidedly the drawing-room music that possesses this popular element, and for this reason it has become such an indispensable adjunct to our social pleasures and home enjoyment. Every other art, painting, poetry, sculpture, shows the same phenomena. There is an innate desire in educated persons to adorn their homes with various objects of art, whether in the realm of painting or sculpture, and that music can contribute to this feeling of home luxury almost more than any other art, simply because it is the luxury most easily attainable, no one will deny. The best specimens of drawing-room music rest on a lyrical foundation; and like every artistic form, drawing-room music has an indisputable right to respectful consideration. Its irresistible charm is to be found in its clear and simple form; in its symmetrical structure, in periods and groupings which may be easily understood, in the short thematic figures to which the composer must strictly keep, and finally, in artistic variations of a pleasing subject, which unfolds the original beauty of the theme, and thus enhances our pleasure. Besides, we find in good drawing-room pieces all possible shades of feeling—sometimes simplicity, grace, melancholy, sometimes again cheerfulness and mirth; and inasmuch as a clear expression of these feelings is too often not immediately recognizable in the larger orchestral works, it is not astonishing, that the general public should cling with such pertinacity to good drawing-room music.

DESCRIPTIVE MUSIC.

I.—TONE-PAINTING.

It is quite natural, that with the unlimited means of characteristic expression possessed by musical art, the composers should have felt the desire to paint, so to speak, by music. Every musical piece that describes and expresses certain feelings of the soul (sometimes such feelings are connected with outward circumstances or events) is in itself a kind of tone-painting; but, in general, we understand, under tone-painting, the endeavor to describe by music visible and tangible objects, appearances of Nature, indeed, all possible outward events and circumstances. All movement is easy to describe, and easiest of all that which in itself possesses a sound. Lord Byron truly says:—

"There's music in all things, if man had ears,
 Their earth is but an echo of the spheres."

"The inner life, the moods and passions of Nature express themselves forcibly in sounds. We hear this music of Nature in the uproar and tumult of the elements, in the rolling and crashing of thunder, in the howling and roaring of the tempest; we hear it in the heart-piercing sounds which the storm draws from the broken rocks; we hear it through the gushing of the foam and the rolling of the mighty sea-waves, in the rippling and bubbling of the stream, and of the rivulet; we hear it in the entire range of the passions, half human in their nature, which animate the higher brute creation; we hear it in the polyphonic warble of the birds, expressive of longing, joy, anger and anxiety; we hear it in the melodious chirping of the grasshopper, exhilarated by the refreshing morning dew."* All these things belong to the audible; among the inaudible but visible are, for instance, high mountains, lofty towers, ruins, etc. These latter frequently offered a subject for musical illustration, or tone-painting. Clement Jannequin, a pupil of Josquin de Prés, selected the noises of the Parisian market-place for the subject of a vocal piece for four parts ("Les Cris de Paris"). Emanuel Bach's "Battle of Hochstädt," and Beethoven's "Battle Symphony" have been preceded by the same Jannequin's victorious Battle of Marignano, of Francis I., against the Swiss. In this battle-piece we hear the signals of the French cavalry, inspiriting calls o' the trumpet, the thunder of the cannon, the whistling and buzzing o' the balls, and at last we hear the despairing cries of the Swiss in their barbarous dialect, "toute frelore la tintclore, toute frelore, bi got." But as this whole battle-scene, with all its terrors and accompaniment of cannon, musketry, etc., is described by human voices, and not by instruments, we may easily imagine that it trenches on the domain of the ludicrous. (Compare for further information the highly interesting essay of C. F. Becker, "Tonmalerei," pp. 40–50, in his book "Die Hausmusik in Deutschland," Leipzig, 1840.) But tone-painting has often been applied in the happiest and most legitimate manner; to cite only a few examples, we would mention the chorus "He spake the word" in Handel's "Israel in Egypt," Beethoven's Pastoral Symphony, the aria for bass "Straight opening" in Haydn's "Creation," etc. These geniuses understood how to keep within the limits of the artistic, and therefore their tone-painting never becomes childish or insipid. In older vocal music "word-painting" was much in fashion. This method aims at giving to the single *word* a musical description, going therefore into the smallest details; for instance, the words "he *descended* from heaven," would be musically described by the descending scale. Such minuteness, although it may satisfy a very painstaking, conscientious composer, affects the whole spirit of the piece in a detrimental manner; it may be called musical pedantry—penny wisdom and pound foolishness.

II.—PROGRAMME MUSIC.

This style was formerly known under the name Symphonià a programma or pittorica. The old programme music professed to give a detailed description of what the composer wishes the public to recognize in his work. As an example we cite the programme of a Sonata for Piano and Violin by Freystädtler (Vienna 1789), called "The Siege of Belgrade," a Turco-historical fantasia: this sonata contains the following descriptive movements:—1. Turkish music in the camp—the soldiers are in readiness—yelling and howling of the Turks; 2. The chaplain gives his blessing; 3. A panic spreads before the advance

---

* E. Pauer's lecture on the "Nature of Music."

of the imperial army—the suburbs are carried by assault; 4. The victors crowned with laurels. The modern composers apply this method without going into these details, and merely point out, by the title given to their symphonies or other instrumental pieces, the matter or subject that suggested the creation of their works. We find, for instance, the Symphonic poems of Liszt describing the following subjects:—1. "Ce qu'on entend sur la montagne" (after Victor Hugo); 2. Tasso, Lament and Triumph; 3. The Preludes (after Lamartine); 4. Orpheus; 5. Prometheus; 6. Mazeppa (after Victor Hugo); 7. Festklänge (festival sounds); 8. Heroide funébre; 9. Hungaria; 10. Hamlet; 11. The Battle of the Huns (after Kulbach's picture); 12. The Ideals (after Schiller). Without pronouncing any opinion as to the desirableness of thus giving a guide to the listener, to indicate what he has actually to imagine himself as hearing, we mention among the universally appreciated and admired examples of programme-music Mendelssohn's descriptive overtures "Hebrides," "Fair Melusina," "Calm Sea and Prosperous Voyage," Sterndale Bennett's overture "Paradise and the Peri," his "Naïades" and the "Wood-nymph," Gade's "Nachklänge von Ossian," and others.

Many names have, however, been given to celebrated pieces by universal consent, and without the concurrence or confirmation of the composer, viz., to various symphonies of Haydn, to Mozart's Symphony in C major, the title "Jupiter;" to the same author's Symphony in E flat, "The Song of the Swan;" to Beethoven's Sonatas, Op. 27, i., "Moonlight Sonata;" to Op. 28, "Pastoral Sonata;" to Op. 31, ii., "Dramatic Sonata;" to Op. 57, the "Storm or Sonata appassionata;" to his Trio, Op. 70, i., the "Ghost Trio;" to his Quartet, Op. 74, the "Harp" Quartet; to his Concerto, No. 5 (Op. 73), the "Emperor's Concerto." The public sentiment is in such instances generally correct, and it would therefore be idle to oppose it; but if such names are given by publishers, without any actual relation to the piece, and merely for the sake of passing off a composition as a novelty just as tailors and milliners give a "taking" title to a coat or a bonnet, the practice is highly reprehensible. (See also foot-notes to Mendelssohn's "Songs without words," and Robert Schumann's Fancy-pieces.)

ROBERT SCHUMANN'S FANCY-PIECES.

Schumann's works form an epoch in the annals of our piano-forte literature; and their great influence may be ascribed to their peculiar intellectual richness and their romantic tendency. He understood how to touch a chord which had not yet been sounded by preceding composers; he presents tone-pictures thoroughly unlike any we have had before—it may be said that there is in each of them a poetical background, which is again the expression of his own personal feeling. Whilst the art of composing was regarded by the composers before Joseph Haydn rather from an outward, objective point of view, the individual, subjective feeling was more and more allowed to penetrate and suffuse the compositions of later masters. As Schumann could, owing to his beginning regular musical studies much later than is ordinarily the case, never obtain such perfect mastery over the musical form, as for instance his contemporary and friend Mendelssohn, it was but natural, that he sought to make up for this deficiency by other means. These means were derived from a decided intellectuality, deep poetical feeling, and a meditative, contemplative disposition.

Certain incidents of Schumann's life were presented in his works, favorite friends were portrayed through musical sounds, and certain melodies—like the old German Grandfather's Dance—may be traced through several of his works. The limits of this book do not allow of any description *in extenso* of Schumann's most celebrated pianoforte works; it must here suffice to call attention to the highly poetical contents of some of them. We begin with his second work, called "Papillons," twelve most beautiful trifles. Of these, Schumann's own interpretation (see Julius Knorr, "Führer auf dem Felde der Clavierunterricht's Litteratur;" Leipzig, Kahnt), p. 69, runs thus: "1. Introductory melody. 2. Imposing impression of the ball-room, gay flickering of the lights. 3. Different parties of masques walk through the room, crossing each other. 4. Harlequin, who mixes freely among the guests. 5. A short polonaise. 6. A scene in the refreshment room; music sounding in the distance from the ball-room. 7, 8. Continuation. 9. Owing to a pause in the music, great confusion among the guests. 10. The guests rearrange themselves in order to resume dancing; an affectionate dialogue in an adjoining room. 11. Grand polonaise, in which the whole company joins. 12. As the end of the ball approaches, the Grandfather's Dance (symbolical of Philistinism and pedantry) resounds: the young people, however, wish to continue their frolic, but at last become tired, and the Grandfather's Dance expressive of the wish of the parents to go home, predominates. The noise of the carnival night dies away. The church clock strikes 'six.' Returned home at last, rest is required, although reminiscences of the pleasant sounds return like an echo." (See also Schumann's letter to Henriette Voigt, in Wasielewski's " Biography of Schumann," p. 340.) With regard to the "Davidsbündler," Op. 6, introduced by the beautiful motto:

> At every turn we find
> Pleasure and pain combined.
> Enjoy with humble mind,
> Endure bravely resigned.

—Schumann says, in the introduction to his "Collected Writings on Music and Musicians" (Leipzig: G. Wiegand, 1854): "And here mention should be made of the society, which was a *more* than secret one, since it only existed in the head of its founder—the Davidsbündler. It seemed not unsuitable, in order to express the various views of art, to invent contrasted artistic characters, of which Florestan and Eusebius were the most prominent, intermediate between whom Meister (Master) Raro stood. This society could be traced, like a red thread, through the newspaper, connecting truth and fiction in a humorous manner." If the "Davidsbund" was originally founded to combat the Philistines Herz, Hünten, and their colleagues, so popular about the year 1830, or to oppose the shallowness of the musical criticism of the period; yet Schumann, as a composer, retained later the form of Florestan and Eusebius in many of his piano-forte works; for like Goethe and other great minds before him, he clearly recognized his dual nature, and separated in himself Florestan, the harsh and wild, from Eusebius, the gentle and mild. It will be seen that the single pieces are signed "F," "E," or "F" and "E." (See also Wasielewski's "Biography of Schumann," pp. 128, 129.) "The Carnival," Op. 9, "scènes mignonnes sur 4 notes," is actually a continuation of the Papillons; here distinct figures are introduced: Pierrot, Pantalon, Columbine, and Harlequin; again, Chopin, Paganini, Chiarina (Clara) Estrella, (Baroness Ernestine de Fricken), and the firm Eusebius and Florestan. The four notes—

are identical with the German names of these notes, A, S, C, H, which together form the name Asch, a small Saxon town on the frontier of Bohemia, in which Mademoiselle de Fricken, a friend of Schumann, resided; besides a, s, c, h, were also the musical letters in Schumann's own name. The celebrated "Phantasiestücke," Op. 12, with their well-chosen titles: 1. Evening; 2. Soaring; 3. Why?; 4. Whims; 5. Night; 6. Fable; 7. Dream Visions; 8. The Climax (Ende vom Lied), are in point of characteristic expression so perfect that no explanation is required. The "Scenes from Childhood," Op. 15, are likewise true and faithful musical pictures. The "Kreisleriana," Op. 16, eight fantasias, were certainly suggested by the "Kreisleriana," Fantasiestücke in Callot's Manier, by E. T. A. Hoffmann (1776–1822). Hoffmann describes in his fragments the sufferings of the Capellmeister Kreisler (a fictitious musician): it is most probable that Schumann, in his highly original and deeply-felt fantasias here portrays his own emotions. The Fantasia, Op. 17, for which he chose as a motto the following lines by Fr. Schlegel:—

> 'Mid all the chords that vibrate through
> Earth's strangely chequered dream,
> There runs a note whose gentle tone
> Is heard aright by him alone
> Who lists with care extreme.

was intended to serve by what it realized, as a contribution towards the fund for erecting Beethoven's monument in Bonn, and Schumann desired to call it "Obolus," and to name the three different movements "Ruins," "Triumphal Arch," and "Crown of Stars." For reasons not known this plan was not carried out. The "Humoreske," which Schumann himself qualifies as a little melancholy, is a kind of suite, in which the dual nature of the composer is again perceptible. The "Novelletten," Op. 21, might be called a continuation of the "Phantasiestücke," Op. 12, only executed with greater freedom, breadth and power. The "Night Visions" (Nachtstücke)—No. 1, mysterious; No. 2, undecided and wavering in its expression; No. 3, recalling the terrors of a thunderstorm; No. 4, an aerial procession of ghosts—were written during a period of great mental anxiety. The "Carnival's Jest from Vienna," Op. 26, is in direct connection with the Papillons and the Carnival, Op. 9. Thus we see that Schumann's piano-forte compositions are more or less suggested by motives not at once apparent to the public. To do real justice to Schumann's interesting works we should remember his own words: "If heaven has bestowed on you a lively imagination, you will often, in solitary hours, sit entranced at the piano, longing to express in harmonies your inward fervor; and the more mystical are your feelings, while you are drawn as it were into magic circles, the more obscure perhaps will the realm of harmony appear."

OBSOLETE FORMS.

Acathistus, a hymn of praise in the Greek Church service; this hymn was sung in honor of the holy Virgin on Saturday before the fifth week of Lent; the congregation was not allowed to be seated during the ceremony.

Anacrusis, Ampeira, Dactyli, Jambicon, Katakeleusinos and *Syrringes* are the parts of the hymn of praise to Apollo, with which candidates strove to gain the prize in the Pythian games.

Crusithyros, a song of the ancient Greeks, which was danced to the accompaniment of flutes.

Dithyrambus, Dithyrambi, among the Greeks were lyrical songs in honor of Bacchus, interspersed with dancing and with instrumental music. Works of this character are distinguished by a wild and unrestrained appearance. We have no authentic specimens of this kind of poetry, but the Phrygian character prevailed in it throughout. A splendid modern example is found in Schubert's setting of Schiller's famous Dithyrambus "Nimmer, das glaubt mir, erscheinen die Götter nimmer allein."

Harmodion, a song which the inhabitants of Athens sung in honor of Harmodius, who delivered them from the yoke of the Pisistratides.

Ithymbos, a dance song of the ancient Greeks in honor of Bacchus. (Compare Dithyrambus.)

Julos, an old Greek hymn, sung by the gleaners in honor of Ceres.

Karaklausithyron, a serenade of the ancient Greeks.

Linos-song, a plaintive song of the ancient Greeks in honor of Linos, a youth of divine descent, who, whilst guarding the sheep, was torn to death by wild dogs. Herodotus found the same song amongst the old Egyptians, who called it *Maneros*, after the name of the son of an Egyptian king. The ancient Greeks sung the Linos-song also during the vintage (see "Iliad," xviii. 567). A similar plaintive was called *Jalemos*.

Prosodion, (a) a song of the ancient Greeks accompanied by instruments; (b) religious songs, dedicated to Apollo and Diana, which were sung as soon as the procession approached the statues of the abovementioned gods, also when the sacrifice was led to the altar.

INDEX.

	PAGE
Acathistus,	171
Accent,	5
" ecclesiastical	16
" grammatical,	6
" oratorical,	16
" transposition of the,	11
Agnus Dei,	58
Air,	109
Allemande,	142
Ambrosian hymn,	57
Ampeira,	172
Amphibrach,	20
Amphimacer,	20
Anacrusis,	172
Anapæst,	21
Angloise,	145
Anthem,	57
Antibacchic,	22
Antiphony,	54
Appendix,	165
Aria,	74
" with or without doubles,	109
Arietta,	78
Arioso,	78
Ave verum corpus,	61
Bacchic,	21
Ballad,	88
Ballade,	88
Ballata,	88
Benedictus,	58
Bergamasca,	158
Bohemian dances,	161
Bolero,	160
Bourrée,	143
Branle,	145
Brawl,	145
Brunette,	88
Burletta,	92
Cachuca,	160
Canon,	47
" apertus,	47
" cancrizans,	51
" clausus,	48
" duplex,	52
" in augmentationem,	51
" in corpo,	48

	PAGE
Canon in diminutionem,	51
" in infinitus,	48
" in the lower seventh,	49
" in the second,	49
" in the upper third,	49
" polymorphus,	50
Canson redonda,	91
Cantata,	82
Cantatina, or Cantatille,	83
Canticum,	61
Canto fermo,	40
Canzone,	91
Canzonetta,	86
Caprice,	136
Capriccio,	137
Carnival,	170
Carnival's Jest from Vienna,	171
Cassazione,	130
Catches,	90
Cavata,	78
Cavatina,	78
Cebell,	143
Chaconne,	145
Chamber-music,	166
Chanson,	87
Chodowe,	162
Chodowska,	161
Choral,	65
" figured,	68
Chorus,	80
Chronological table of opera composers,	100
Coloratura,	79
Concerted pieces,	95
Concertino,	134
Concerto,	132
" di camera,	132
" da chiesa,	70
" grosso,	109
Concert overture,	135
Concertstück,	134
Contredanse,	161
Convivial songs,	89
Cossak,	162
Counterpoint,	40
" double,	42
Country-dance,	156
Couplet,	90

INDEX.

	PAGE
Courante (Corrente),	143
Cracoviac,	163
Cretic,	22
Crusithyros,	172
Csárdás,	163
Cushion-dance,	156
Cyclical forms,	112
Dactyl,	21, 172
Dance movements classified with respect to their time and rhythmical expression,	148
" music,	142
" tunes,	110
Dances, modern and national,	155
" Bohemian,	161
" English,	156
" French,	161
" German,	155
" Hungarian,	163
" Italian,	158
" Moldavian,	157
" Norwegian,	157
" (old),	142
" Polish,	163
" Roumanian,	157
" Russian,	162
" Spanish,	159
" Swedish,	157
" Wallachian,	157
Danses de cérémonie,	163
Davidsbündler,	170
Descriptive music,	167
Dialogo (dialogue),	80
Dithyramb, dithyrambus,	172
Divertimento,	130
Dramatic scene,	94
Drawing-room music,	167
Duet,	79
" chamber,	79
" dramatic,	80
Duodrama,	165
Ecclesiastical accent,	16
Eclogue,	141
Ecossaise,	161
English dances,	156
Ensemble pieces,	95
Esquisse,	142
L'Eté,	161
Etude,	141
Fancy pieces (Robert Schumann's),	169
Fandango,	160
Fantasia,	136
Festival overture,	135
Figure,	27
Figured choral,	68
Finale of opera,	95
" of sonata,	114
Form in music,	5

	PAGE
Forms belonging to sacred and secular vocal music,	71
" cyclical,	112
" of movements,	54
" sacred,	54
" secular,	86
" single,	136
" with regard to the relation of separate parts of polyphonic music,	40
French dances,	161
" opéra comique,	97
Fris,	164
Fugue,	43, 108
Gagliardo, Gaillarde, Galliard,	147
Gavotte,	143
German dances,	155
Gigue,	144
Gitana,	160
Glee,	90
Golubez,	162
Gradual,	59
Grammatical accent,	6
Ground,	109
Harmodion,	172
Heavy dactyls,	23
" spondees,	22
Hopping dance,	157
Hornpipe,	156
Humoreske,	171
Humorous songs,	89
Hungarian dances,	163
Husitska,	162
Hymn,	56
" Ambrosian,	57
Iambic,	19
Idyll,	141
Impromptu,	141
Instrumental music,	104
Intermedium,	99
Intermezzo,	99, 141
Intrade,	108
Intrata,	108
Introduction,	108
Introit,	59
Invention,	107
Italian dances,	158
Ithymbos,	172
Jambicon,	172
Jota arragoneza,	160
Julos,	172
Karaklausithyron,	172
Katakeleusinos,	172
Kreisleriana,	171

	PAGE
Lai,	91
Lamentations,	61
Lancers, Lanciers,	161
Ländler,	162
Lassan, Lassú,	163
Lauda Sion salvatorem,	61
Laudes,	62
" episcopi,	62
Laudi spirituali,	62
Lay,	91
Leich,	91
Lied,	86
Liederspiel,	92
Liedertafeln,	89
Linos-song,	172
Love-songs,	87
Madrigal,	90
Madrilena,	160
Maggiolata,	88
Magnificat,	61
Maneros,	172
March,	138
" aux flambeaux,	163
" funeral,	140
" national,	140
" quick,	138
" religious,	140
" slow,	140
" triumphal or festival,	140
Mass,	58
" funeral,	58
Masque,	92
Maypole dance,	156
Mazurek, Mazurka,	163
Measure (dance),	156
Mélange,	142
Melodrama,	165
Melody,	29
Metre,	18
Metres, table of different, as applied in music,	18
Minuet, menuet,	146
Miserere,	60
Modern dances,	155
Moldavian dances,	157
Molossus,	22
Monferina,	158
Monodrama,	165
Motet,	58
Movements, forms of,	54
Musetta,	143
Nachtstücke,	171
National dances,	155
" songs,	89
Night-visions,	171
Noëls,	88
Norwegian dances,	157
Notturno,	130
Novelletten,	171

	PAGE
Obsolete forms of songs,	91
" forms,	171
Offertory,	60
Old dances,	142
Opera,	92
" English (ballad),	98
" German (romantic),	98
" French (comique),	97
" Italian,	97
Oratorio,	62
Oratorical accent,	16
Overture,	134
" artistic,	135
" concert,	135
" French,	134
" Italian,	135
" opera,	135
" plan of older,	135
" programme,	135
Pantalon,	161
Papillons,	170
Partita,	110
Passacaglio, Passecaille, Passagallo,	146
Passamezzo,	146
Passepied,	147
Passion-Music,	63
Pasticcio,	142
Pastourelle,	161
Pastoral,	92
Pavan,	147
Period, the, and its construction,	33
Phantasiestücke,	171
Plan of Beethoven's Sonata, Op. 53.	
Polish dances,	163
Polka,	162
Polonaise,	163
Potpourri,	142
Poule,	161
Prelude,	106
Programme-music,	167
Prosodion,	172
Psalmody,	69
Psalms,	69
Pyrrhic,	20
Quadrille,	161
Quartet, string,	130
Quintet,	130
Quodlibet,	84, 142
Recitative,	71
Reel,	156
Rejdowák,	162
Requiem,	58
Rhapsody,	141
Rhythm,	23
Ricercata,	107
Rigaudon, Rigadoon,	147

	PAGE		PAGE
Rondo,	115	Sousedska,	162
" form of,	115	Spanish dances,	159
Roumanian dances,	157	Spondee,	20
Rounds,	90	Springdans,	157
Russian dances,	162	Stabat Mater,	60
Russjaka,	162	Stilo concertate,	106
		String quartet,	130
Sacred cantata,	82	Structure of the grand aria,	75
" forms,	54	Study,	141
" songs,	87	Style,	25
Saltarello,	158	Suite,	109
Salve regina,	61	Swedish dances,	157
Sarabande,	144	Symphony,	131
Scene, the dramatic,	94	" old,	108
Scherzo,	137	" modern,	131
Schottisch,	161	Syrringes,	172
Secular forms,	86		
Seguidillas,	159	Tarantella,	158
Sentimental dance,	158	Terzett,	94
Serenade,	130	Thematic work,	38
Siciliano,	147	Toccata,	107
Single forms,	136	Tone-painting,	167
Skávavá,	162	Trásák,	161
Sketch,	142	Trénise,	161
Skizze,	142	Tribrach,	22
Sonata,	112	Trio,	94
" form of,	113	Triumphal march,	144
" form of finale,	114	" overture,	135
" " first movement,	113	Trochee,	18
" " scherzo,	114		
" " slow movement,	113	Umrlec,	162
" solo,	117		
Song,	86	Variation,	137
Songs, convivial,	89	Villanella,	141
" humorous,	89	Voluntary,	107
" love,	87		
" national,	89	Wallachian dances,	157
" without words,	140	Walzer,	155

www.ingramcontent.com/pod-product-compliance
Lightning Source LLC
Chambersburg PA
CBHW020257170426
43202CB00008B/409